WORLD
through
My Window

Rabbi Erwin Schild

ADATH ISRAEL CONGREGATION
Toronto, Canada

Typesetting and page layout by Design Oriented.

FIRST EDITION

Canadian Cataloguing in Publication Data

Schild, Erwin, 1920-
    World through My Window

Includes index.
ISBN 0-9696226-0-0

1. Jewish sermons. 2. Jewish sermons, Canadian (English).* I. Adath Israel Congregation (Toronto, Ont.). II. Title.

BM740.2.S33 1992   296.4'2   CP2-094243-1

To the memory of

My parents, HERMANN and HETTI SCHILD,

My brother, KURT SCHILD

My sister, MARGOT SCHUSTER;

and

To my WIFE, LAURA, for LOVE, FAITH and PATIENCE

זכרתי לך חסד נעוריך אהבת כלולתיך
לכתך אחרי במדבר בארץ לא זרועה

I remember the devotion of your youth,
Your love as a bride,
How you followed me through the wilderness,
In a land not sown.
                                                    (Jeremiah 2:2)

and

To my CHILDREN and GRANDCHILDREN, for Hope Renewed.

The MAP

Table of CONTENTS

The First Window

The Second Window

The Third Window

The Fourth Window

Foreword

Growing up Jewish in the Toronto of 1940s and 50s was special. It was, of course, difficult because of the pervasive anti-Semitism of the times, yet one of the real treats I still vividly relish was the occasional Sabbath or holiday when my father would skip services at our tiny hole-in-the-wall synagogue on Cecil Street and take me to what I then perceived as the majestic, cavernous Adath Israel Congregation on Bathurst Street. Actually as I look back now, I realize that the sanctuary was probably the size of a small school auditorium, but in those days it was imposing. But more importantly it had a new young rabbi my father was anxious to hear.

And what a wonder that rabbi was to me. Not the venerable, bearded, rigid rabbi I was accustomed to, speaking words I did not understand. Rather, here was a modern, handsome young man who – unusual at the time, at least for orthodox rabbis – spoke English. His sermons were always crisp, comprehensible, and even to my young ears, beautifully crafted. For the first time, he made going to shul more a joy than a job. That was my introduction some forty years ago to Erwin Schild.

Over the years I never forgot those early memories. When I was at the University of Toronto I would take Jewish students in residence to services at the Adath Israel – simply to hear Rabbi Schild.

He never disappointed. Whatever the question, whatever the issue, whatever the crisis, Rabbi Schild had an answer. He was original, refreshing and made wonderful use of the English language; indeed, he used the language in ways few of us thought possible. So impressive was he, and so taken were my friends with him, that in later years when they settled in Toronto many joined his congregation.

Rabbi Schild's story is an inspiring one. Born and educated in Germany, imprisoned in Dachau after Krystallnacht he somehow managed to make his way to England as a young student. When war broke out a year later, despite the fact that he was both a teenager and Jewish, he was rounded up by the British government as an "enemy alien" and shipped off to a detention camp in Canada with Nazi prisoners-of-war. Eventually he was released and finished his studies at the University of Toronto and at Rabbi Price's famous yeshiva where he was ordained. The rest is history.

To me Erwin Schild is the most poignant symbol of an opportunity missed. At a time in the 1930s and early 40s when so many hundreds of thousands of European Jews were on the move looking for a sanctuary to escape the murderous Nazis, Canada turned its back. No western country had a worse record in accepting Jewish refugees than ours. Only because he was a British prisoner was a young Erwin Schild along with several thousand other Jewish internees admitted into Canada. And what a remarkable contribution these men – many of whom settled in Canada – were to make to their adopted homeland. They became over the years, leaders of this country's scientific, artistic, academic and literary communities. And no one contributed more to this country than Erwin Schild.

As a theologian, as a passionate crusader for social justice, as a fierce fighter for the oppressed, as a staunch proponent of Israel and an eloquent spokesman for Canadian Jewry, Erwin Schild has made his mark on this country. He was a gift to this country from both a depraved German government and paranoid British government – a gift only reluctantly accepted by an anti-Semitic Canadian government, a gift for which a new generation of Canadians would be eternally grateful.

In this book you will find Erwin Schild at his very best. Whether discussing religion, the Holocaust, Israel, life and death, his words are magic – at the same time both soothing and inspiring. Who can fail to be touched as he bids farewell to his close friend of many years Albert Pappenheim and comforts us for the loss at the hands of a cruel terrorist on a Tel-Aviv beach, of the vibrant Marni Kimelman; or when he writes about his love for his new home Canada, and his passion for the home of all Jews, Israel; or when he describes his return to his birthplace, Germany.

This is a book that ought to be cherished and savoured, read and reread. It stands as a tribute to a great humanitarian, a great Canadian and a great Jew. Above all, it reminds us of why we are so much in his debt.

Irving Abella
Professor of History,
York University
President, Canadian Jewish Congress

ix

Publisher's Preface

You are about to read the literary distillation of a forty-year relationship between a Rabbi and his Congregation. It is difficult to capture, in a few words, the essence of the devotion, intellectual challenge and spiritual comfort that has permeated Rabbi Erwin Schild's ministry.

This book will undoubtedly refresh old memories for some readers, yet open new perspectives for others.

Adath Israel Congregation is privileged to have participated in the publication of this volume in order to share with the reader some of the messages which have inspired us.

Alan Applebaum, President
Adath Israel Congregation
April 1992

Thanks!
A Prefatory Acknowledgement

ברוך ה' אשר חונן לאדם דעת ומלמד לאנוש בינה

With thanks to the Almighty "Who grants knowledge to human beings and teaches mortals insight," I rejoice at the publication of my book "World through My Window."

My joy goes beyond the happiness one feels at the successful conclusion of an exciting project. My joy springs from a deep source of gratitude. I am grateful that at least some of my sermons have been snatched from the black hole of oblivion in which sermons generally disappear after they have been prepared, delivered, discussed and forgotten.

Sermons are so ephemeral. What trace remains of the more than two thousand sermons I have preached in the course of my rabbinate? They represent a good portion of my labour, my working time, my spiritual energy and my creative effort. Yet each sermon was heard only by a fraction of the people whom I would have liked to reach and whom I had in mind when I prepared my message. Even when I preached in a crowded Synagogue on a Festival or High Holy Day, those who needed the sermon most may not have been there to hear it!

Sermons are spoken words: fleeting, ethereal. No matter how weighty the subject, how deep the thought, how eloquent the delivery and how receptive the listener, the word is heard no more. The effect may endure; a response may have been evoked; a change may have been triggered and a life touched, yet the sermon evanesced. It went to oblivion.

To convert thirty or so of my sermons - chosen rather randomly, perhaps in optimistic anticipation of future volumes - into a printed book, an abiding literary document, is therefore a cause of deep joy and grateful satisfaction for me.

I am indebted to a number of individuals who were instrumental in the publication of my book.

My financial patrons who provided the funding for the production of this book and its distribution to the members of Adath Israel Congregation are acknowledged in a separate tribute. I trust my readers will share my appreciation for their generosity and public spirit.

In this preface, I would like to thank the individuals who have contributed their time, their skills and expertise, their critical faculty and, above all, their encouragement.

Mr. Stephen Gibson, owner of Concord Publishing Co. and a Synagogue member who has listened to my sermons regularly for many years, gave me encouragement to publish my sermons and promised his professional assistance in the editorial and technical production as a labour of love. He kept his promise. He was one of a group of volunteers and friends which included David Feldman who accepted responsibility for the cover design and page layout. Other members of this group were Abe Fish, Paul and Nellie Jacobs, Gail Kaufman, Marilyn Rosenzweig and Marlene Walker. They read and corrected the manuscript at different stages, offered suggestions and critiques, planned publicity and "marketing" and by sharing, spread enthusiasm and created excitement.

Special thanks are due to Beatrice Solomon, my loyal and resourceful co-worker at my Synagogue for more than 35 years. Her tireless efforts, sensitive judgement, good sense, experience and wisdom were indispensable to the preparation and production of my book. I hope my debt of gratitude to Bea will be reduced in some measure by her joy in seeing the book completed. I hope that all my other co-workers and supporters will feel similarly rewarded.

I would like to express appreciation to Edith Land, a Christian friend and frequent collaborator. She contributed valuable advice to enhance the usefulness and relevance of the book for the Christian and general community.

I extend my gratitude to Alan Applebaum, president of my Synagogue, Adath Israel, its officers and Board of Governors, for undertaking the publication of "World through My Window."

Last but not least, my thanks to my long-term colleagues, Cantor A. Eliezer Kirshblum and Sexton Alex Koenigsberg, and to all the worshippers at Adath Israel Synagogue: the men, women and children whose praise, compliments, criticism and warmth were constant incentives for me to put my best into every sermon!

I pray to God for continued life, health, energy and creativity to learn, think, speak, teach and write.

In Grateful Recognition

I would like to acknowledge with profound appreciation the generous support of individuals and families whose material contribution made the publication of this book by Adath Israel Congregation possible.

Doris and Morris G. Adams
Michael and Penny Benjamin
Beverley and Sam Cohen
Alice and Alex Davis
Saul and Ruth Ellis
Mr. & Mrs. Eric Exton
Abe and Marcy Fish
Carol and Herman Gottesman
Rina and Irving Gottesman
Florence and Harold Lazar
Morris and Alice Macarz
Martin and Judith Markus and Family
Gerald and Karen Papernick
Harry L. Romberg and Sara L. Romberg
Victor and Rhoda Shields
Abby J. Sone and Family in memory of Dr. Dorothy Sone
Janet and Allen Werger, Jerry and Shelley Werger
and Belle Werger

Their magnanimous gift is a testimony to friendship and loyalty. I am honoured and encouraged by their faith and trust.

Rabbi Erwin Schild
II Adar, 5752 - March 1992

A Reader's Guide to
"World through My Window"

Sermons are preached one at a time. Before the rabbi preaches, he must make a choice: from the profusion of issues, causes and problems he would like to address, from the plethora of ideas and themes he would like to share, he must select one subject.

Hopefully, in the course of a year or two or three, the rabbi will have led his congregation through the universe of his concerns. He will have defined his positions on current and perennial issues and tried to move the members of his audience in his direction. He will also in due course address subjects of relatively minor urgency and return to some of his topics - those he deems most important - more often than to others.

In selecting the sermons for "World through My Window," I did not attempt a systematic or comprehensive presentation of my ideology. I chose sermons which for some reason I was particularly anxious to share with my readers. The book has no plot with a beginning, development and finish. Each sermon stands on its own. None is the sequel of, or prelude to, the other.

Thus, there were no compelling criteria by which to arrange the sequence of the material. Several themes appear more than once, such as the State of Israel, Jewish Life, the Holocaust and the problems of contemporary living. This simply reflects the priorities of my preaching. The division of the book in four parts allows for the separation of multiple treatments of similar themes and enables us to take another look through the window from a different perspective.

Thus it is not necessary to read the book in any particular order.

For my readers' guidance, I have included a Map of the World through My Window. If you choose to follow the suggested order and to start at the beginning, you will find in the First Window a panorama of themes that had, and still have, a high degree of priority in the hierarchy of my values. The Second Window, in a certain sense, is retrospective. The sermons and addresses in this part were generated by passages in my private life and events on the communal and world scene. However, regardless of their time-conditioned origin, the ideas or memories preserved in this section remain meaningful now and in the future. The sermons displayed in the Third Window are held together by my hope that they may help readers to face a number of private and public perplexities. The Fourth Window is a collection of sermons and addresses which try to define my approach to some existential questions that I must answer as the person I am. I invite those with whom I share time and place to look through this window with me.

Despite this rationale for the structure of "World through My Window," readers may plot their own route through this world. You may want to know what I have to say about the State of Israel, or about the Holocaust or my relations to Germany. You may want to read what approach I recommend to certain crises in life or certain problems of faith and religious thought. The Map should help you find what you are looking for. Near the end of the book, you will also find an "Index" which you will find useful to spot particular topics. If Hebrew words, names or unfamiliar expressions puzzle you, please refer to the "Glossary."

Above all, I hope your visit to the "World through My Window" will be interesting and stimulating. May you find incentives for thought and action!

NOTE ON TRANSLITERATION
In transliterating Hebrew, we have aimed at ease of pronunciation and word recognition rather than philological accuracy.

World through My Window
an Introduction

A room without windows is not a suitable place for prayer. Thus teaches our Jewish tradition. [1]

If prayer – a communion between the worshipper and God – calls for a room with a view, then the study in which the preacher prepares his sermon must be even more exposed to the world and have a window open to the human soul.

What is the difference between a lecture and a sermon?

A lecture addresses a subject. A sermon, however, should address people. A sermon is not an academic examination of a topic, but an attempt to change the attitude of the listeners, to influence their actions, and to change lives. Whether the change hoped for is modest or radical, whether it pertains to religious observance, ethical conduct or personal character, a sermon is an appeal that calls for a response.

Therefore, the rabbi, minister, or priest cannot live in an ivory tower. He needs a window on the world. He has to deal with present human conditions and contemporary issues. He must interpret current events and trends in order to influence his listeners' responses.

A Jewish sermon, in addition, must be "Torah," authentic Jewish teaching. The rabbi interprets the Jewish tradition and its literature, while he interprets life and the world. He does not look through the window with the detachment of a neutral observer, but he refracts the world through the prism of Torah.

The rabbi should not claim the role of the licensed authoritative spokesperson for Torah. That would be presumptuous. The Torah addresses each of us differently according to our individual capacity and receptiveness. The rabbi hopes that by virtue of his diligent study of Torah the thoughts he articulates will be Torah thoughts emanating from the sources he utilizes and from the tradition he has studied. He hopes that his sermons will illuminate the darkness of the world and the darkness of the human soul through the light of Torah, however dimly it may shine through him. Even this modest hope imposes a grave responsibility on the rabbi.

Sermons reflect history. They ought to be read against the background of their moment in time, as they react to changes in the world or anticipate impending developments.

In addition, when the Rabbi deals with problems of the individual and crises of human life, he is bound to be referring to his own self. In fact, the Rabbi's best sermons are probably those in which he wrestles with the human reality he shares with his listeners.

This collection of sermons therefore incorporates history and autobiography.

The sermons were selected from notes accumulated over the forty-two years during which I was privileged to preach to Adath Israel Congregation as its senior rabbi, and afterwards as Rabbi Emeritus. The first sermon I preached as rabbi of Adath Israel of Toronto, in September 1947, dealt with the desperate struggle of the Jewish people for its homeland, and particularly with the drama of the ship "Exodus," then beginning to unfold. My first sermon as Rabbi Emeritus, on Rosh Hashana 1989, against the background of my retirement, addressed the critical problem of change in the life of the individual.

In presenting these selected sermons, I have tried to indicate their historical and biographical context so as to make them more meaningful for the reader. Older readers will refresh historical memories, while younger ones may try to see the past through my window. Both young and old, I hope, will discover insights relevant not only to the understanding of the past, but also to our life in the present time and to our expectations for the future.

I hope that looking through my window, the reader will perceive, among all the things that are personal and changing, at least a fleeting image of the universal and the eternal.

Erwin Schild

March 1992 - Adar II 5752

1 *"A person should pray only in a house with windows"* (Talmud Brachot 34b)

The FIRST window

Is Life Worthwhile?

Both reason and emotion must be involved in the making of a sermon. Naturally, the balance of heart and mind is not always even.

The sermon "Is Life Worthwhile?" was obviously dictated by my heart. It is not a rational systematic exposition of my philosophy of life. It is an impressionistic collage of reveries, memories, and insights.

Nevertheless, I did not preach this sermon on Yom Kippur of 5752 as a personal catharsis. "Words coming from the heart can enter the heart" is a popular Jewish proverb. I hoped that by laying bare an inner experience of mine I would encourage my congregants in their own search for meaning and for values that make life worthwhile.

Is Life Worthwhile?
A sermon preached before Yizkor on Yom Kippur 5752 - 1991

A strange transformation came over me in the interval between my Bar Mitzvah and my sister's eleventh birthday six weeks later. At my Bar Mitzvah party, everything had been normal: the boys teased the girls while the girls whispered secrets in one another's ears to make the boys mad. When the same group got together to celebrate my sister's birthday, I had mysteriously changed. I had eyes and ears only for one girl, Ruth, 13 years old. How she had blossomed to young womanhood! I had noticed it during the preceding weeks. I felt swept away by emotions I had never known before.

A beautiful friendship ensued, utterly innocent and romantic. We sought each other's company whenever we could. We were rarely alone, but when the kids got together at play, at parties, in the Synagogue, at someone's home, on hikes and sometimes at the

3

swimming pool, we were always together. We talked a lot about love in the abstract, and about other ideals, such as truth, loyalty, beauty and justice, but we never had the temerity to say that we were in love with each other. We compared school work; we read the same books and on the occasional walk by ourselves we pretended to be heroes from the adventure novels we both liked to read.

When the teenage romance eventually faded, we remained true friends and mutual confidants. But those were difficult years of growing up as Jews under the Hitler regime in Germany. Our ways parted: I found refuge in England, and Ruth eventually made her way to Holland where unfortunately the Germans caught up with her again.

Once during the war I received a message from Ruth through the International Red Cross. It said that Ruth was working at a hospital in Amsterdam. I never heard from her again. Her one surviving sister, who lives in New Jersey and with whom we have been very close all these years, found out that Ruth was deported to Auschwitz where she perished at 23 years of age.

I have a persistent fantasy which captures my imagination again and again. My life is over -many years hence, I hope- and I arrive in the beyond, bent with age, wounded and scarred from the battles of life. And there I will meet Ruth: young, virginal, shining with the radiance of a sainted martyr. She will be waiting to ask me a question:

"Erwin, tell me, please! Did I miss anything? Was it really worthwhile? What did I miss?"

My fantasy is nourished by a famous passage in the Talmud (Eruvin 13b):

> *For two and a half years, the Schools of Shammai and Hillel were divided. One school argued: It were better [1] if man had not been created rather than that he was created. Their opponents argued: It is better that man was created rather than if he had not been created. Finally they took a vote and decided: better if man had not been created! But now that he was created, let him examine his deeds!*

If we could only have a transcript of this debate! Imagine, a dispute lasting for two and a half years on the question whether life is worthwhile! Is life a benefit or a burden? A detriment or a privilege?

4

And by which criteria are we to examine our deeds? What are the deeds or experiences that make life worthwhile?

I would have cast my ballot for the positive. A few years ago, a peculiar experience confirmed for me the worth of living.

There is a word for an experience of the kind that I so vividly remember: epiphany. An epiphany is a sudden intuitive insight into the reality of a situation or its essential meaning, usually triggered by an ordinary occurrence or circumstance.

I had an epiphany in January of 1968.

My wife Laura and I were about to leave for the Toronto airport on our first visit to the State of Israel.

The poignancy of the moment was heightened for me by the awareness that this was also the first time for me to leave the North American continent since I had arrived in Canada twenty-eight years before as an interned refugee, a prisoner to all intents and purposes.

On the preceding Shabbat I had spoken in my Synagogue of my anticipations: how excited I was looking forward to setting foot on the sovereign Jewish homeland; how I would approach the Western Wall as an emissary of my parents, grandparents, and all the generations who never had the privilege of a pilgrimage to the Holy Land; how I would carry the heavy baggage of history and how I would be proxy for all the members of my congregation.

I was standing in front of our house when our 21-year-old daughter Judith, a student at the University of Toronto, was backing our car out of the garage.

That scene -that very moment- brought everything together for me: my background and my past, my marriage, our family, our home, our share of material prosperity represented by the fine automobile my daughter was about to drive to the airport; my love for the State of Israel which we were at last going to visit; the optimistic excitement for Israel's future after her triumph in the recent Six-Day War; our gratitude for friendships we cherished, for we were travelling together with dear friends; the role of Adath Israel Synagogue in our lives and my place in the congregation, for our travelling companions were none other than the Synagogue president and his wife.

In a flash, this epiphany revealed to me the goodness of my life. My life had such meaning! I could perceive the sources of my happiness and blessedness.

A wave of joy swept over me.

I felt rewarded for my labours in the congregation that represented my life's work; I felt grateful for working with Jewish values, for planting seeds of love for Torah and for the Jewish people. How gratifying to be able to combine this meaningful work with personal fulfilment through family and friendship!

It would be vulgar if I were to parade my life in public. Yet I want to challenge every one of you with the same question that was answered for me at that moment. What makes your life worth living? What justifies your privilege of being alive, a privilege taken away from so many? Can you validate what you do, your work and your personal goals, and can you say: It is better I was created than if I were not?

To justify our lives we must be able to speak of love; of having found the person with whom we wanted to share our lives; of marriage and of family. We may want to speak of holding our child in our arms, of watching first steps taken and of hearing first words spoken. And if one has no child, one must have heard and understood God's assurance to the childless in the Book of Isaiah (56:5) *"I shall give them in my house and within my walls 'yad vashem' -perpetual renown- better than sons and daughters."* Our participation in the work of the people Israel and our effect on the human community are assurance of meaning and perpetuity.

To justify our lives we must be able to speak of friendship, of the giving of self to others and of our willingness to receive in return.

Joy makes life worthwhile. Living ought to be suffused with a spiritual sensitivity, a "high" that is not an isolated peak but an abiding elevation. If we are fortunate, we experience the joy of good health and of happy events. Yet the sources of joy are almost innumerable: a sunset over the ocean, the sight of snow-capped mountains, the bliss of listening to music, the delight from reading a book or a poem, the feeling of growing beyond ourselves in the contemplation of a painting, a walk on a beach, a run through a park or the exhilaration of a downhill ski.

The joy of being Jewish makes life worthwhile: to celebrate life and

6

to hallow it through Mitzvot, to enhance the ordinary through the spiritual, to cling to God through Torah and to embrace the eternal community of Israel.

There is another facet of life which gives it worth, uniqueness and meaning: to witness history and to participate in it.

What a century we were destined to live in! History has no parallel for the twentieth century and no precedent for the incredible changes which have taken place in it. The argument that former times may have brought similarly rapid developments is specious. Means of communications available in earlier centuries were primitive. News, or rather rumours, spread slowly and sporadically. People had few opportunities of being witnesses to contemporary events. How long would it have taken for a settler in northern Quebec to hear of the Battle of Waterloo?

Modern means of communications, most of which were developed in this century, have linked the whole world into one instantaneous network. This very fact exerts a tremendous influence on the unfolding of events and accelerates the pace of history. A veritable cataract of historic events, including the recent astounding developments in Eastern Europe, has thundered down on us.

We have had front row seats in the theatre of history and many of us have been bit-players in the dramatic spectacle.

The Jewish people have been in the focus of world events for at least the past fifty years. Some of us lived through the humiliation of the "Jewish Question" in the '20s and '30s, when we were disheartened by the unexpected survival of anti-Semitism in a scientific and presumably enlightened age. We experienced the Holocaust. Emerging from the ordeal of genocide, we witnessed the greatest saving miracle of our history: the rise of the State of Israel. We have since been participants in the ongoing miracle of Israel's survival.

The ingathering of Jews from the Soviet Union is of momentous significance and one of the star events of the recent past. It is history at its most exciting! The success of the State of Israel in snatching Ethiopian Jews, long separated members of the ancient House of Israel, from the brink of oblivion is a further instance of Jewish history erupting with explosive speed before our very eyes.

History has given our lives a unique dimension. Life, turbulent and painful as it was, has been full and deep: a gripping, exciting adventure.

I know, therefore, what I must tell my friend Ruth.

With deep sadness, with endless regret and with profound compassion I must say: "Yes, Ruth, you did miss something! You missed - everything! How sad that you were denied the indescribable privilege of living! How sad you were deprived of Life in our Time! Yes, my life has been worthwhile."

Will she not then ask another question?

"Did my death make much difference in your life? Did millions of deaths like mine affect the lives of your lucky contemporaries? Did it influence and change their glorious, beautiful, meaningful lives?"

That question I cannot answer by myself. It hangs over us all. I can only say that I did remember her and all my other friends, and that I dedicated a corner of my life to them.

We all can and do remember.

But did remembrance really affect and change us? Did we learn anything from the needless deaths? Did we learn at least to be devoted to the State of Israel?

Had there been a Jewish state in the '30s, Ruth and all my other lost friends and relatives would have been saved. The Holocaust would not have happened to us; it could happen only to a homeless people!

The world persists on its course of rapid change. The road ahead, as always, is unpredictable and may turn and twist more abruptly than ever. But one thing is certain for the Jewish people: we need the State of Israel. In the presence of our sacred memories, we know that we owe it to our martyrs to support Israel. To build it sound, strong and secure helps make our lives worthwhile.

---

[1] *The Hebrew adjective used in the text carries nuances that are difficult to reproduce in one English word. It means "easier, more advantageous, more beneficial, less problematic."*

God: Male and/or Female?

No other problem has monopolized the attention of Conservative Judaism as constantly as the place of women in Jewish religious life. Almost from its very inception, the Conservative Movement wrestled with the dilemma of female inequality in Jewish family law. Conservative Judaism sought to redress the inequities that created extraordinary hardships and were repugnant to contemporary sensibilities.

There is no denying that the social and legal system of Judaism is male-oriented. Only adult Jewish males are the fully participating members of the religious community. Women, respected for a role of their own, are honoured and protected, but confined to a sphere apart.

As women successfully strove for equality in secular society, the pressure increased to eliminate the barriers which excluded women from full participation in the Jewish religious life. At least in our community, the removal of the "Mechitza," the separation between men and women during worship, became the distinguishing mark of the Conservative Synagogue. It was the single most effective innovation to make the Conservative Synagogue popular in the post-war period.

However, the cause of women's rights in the Synagogue could not rest there.

Though few people realized it, the function of the Mechitza was not primarily to separate the sexes but to separate the spectators, i.e. the women, from the participants in the service, namely the men. Once the Mechitza had fallen and at the same time the unfortunate circumstance had arisen that most men had become so ignorant of Jewish ritual that they could no longer really participate, there was no longer a credible rationale for keeping the roles of men and women in the Synagogue apart. Both men and women were mere spectators to the ritual conducted by professional personnel. The few who were fortunate enough to be able to participate, due to their upbringing and education, were men and women in equal proportion. Perhaps even, women might have had the edge in the Conservative Synagogue.

Thus, a conflict between the egalitarian thrust and the conventional status quo became inevitable. This conflict still continues within many Synagogues. Men and women demanded that equal rights be given to women to be counted for the "Minyan," as well as to Aliyot, the honour of being called to the Torah.

One concession had been made long ago to women even by the more precedent-bound streams within Judaism: equal access to quality Jewish education. Few educational institutions discriminated to any significant degree between the subjects taught to boys and girls respectively. Though some marginal differentiation was observed, even Orthodoxy by and large offered and promoted quality Jewish education for girls and encouraged women to continue Torah study as part of their Jewish lives.

In general, the opening of Jewish learning to women did not still demands for wider participation in the ritual life, except possibly in the Orthodox community. Even there, the new phenomenon of Women's Minyanim, worship service by and for women only, made its controversial appearance.

We know in which direction the Conservative community moved. Congregations were encouraged to count women for the "Minyan," the quorum required for communal worship, and call women to the Torah reading. Ordination to the rabbinate and the cantorate were to follow. Egalitarianism has been ascendant.

For some women, the quest for equal worship opportunity was not primarily a religious issue but an application to the Synagogue of the feminist principle of equality which they passionately espoused. For many other women in our Conservative community, however, the quest was motivated by the need to express a genuine religious commitment. Many women felt that the bounds of the conventionally accepted woman's role were too narrow to accommodate their personal Jewish piety and their search for Jewish spirituality. It was tragic for the quality of debate that this aspect of the conflict was often deliberately ignored, or misunderstood. The protagonists of the status quo preferred to view the conflict in terms of loyalty to Halacha and Tradition on one side versus reform and contempt of Tradition on the other.

More thoughtful critics of ritual egalitarianism may argue that the erosion of role differentiation between men and women in modern society may jeopardize the traditional Jewish family structure. It may have undesirable social, psychological and demographic consequences. As wife and mother, the woman holds an important position in the family that cannot be easily delegated.

Egalitarianism, therefore, is an issue that must be discussed with respect and sensitivity. I have tried to do so in several sermons at various times. My most comprehensive treatment of the subject was reserved for Kol Nidre night, 1986.

God: Male and/or Female?
A Sermon preached on Kol Nidre Night 5747 - 1986

Yom Kippur is a day of reconciliation. It gives us courage to try to heal the breach between God and ourselves and to remove the barriers separating human beings from one another.

One of the great rifts running through our world divides the two halves of humanity: male and female. The growth of feminism and the transformations of the conventional roles of men and women provoke angry confrontations. Passion and paranoia deepen the division. Forces in our individual and social psyche seem to be pulling men and women apart.

Religion is deeply involved in the struggle between the sexes. It is one of the battlefields on which the antagonists clash. The stability of the Catholic Church has been shaken by women's demands for equality. Priesthood for women is still controversial in the Anglican Church. In the Jewish community, the issues of female ordination and egalitarian worship continue to roil the tempers and are far from resolved.

Another possible involvement of religion in the gender conflict is even more serious.

11

Does religion, and Judaism in particular, nourish sexual prejudice? Is religion a breeding ground of male chauvinism? Has religion been a willing accomplice in the conspiracy to keep women second-class members of society? Has Judaism helped create the tradition of female subordination and has it retarded the achievement of equality?

If I were a woman, I might resent that God is continuously addressed as *"Avinu Malkeinu - our Father, our King,"* but never as our Mother. I might feel denigrated by the constant reference to God as "He," never as "She."

Our theologians insist that in God there is neither maleness nor femaleness. God has no body, no physical properties. A non-corporeal Being, he is without biological attributes. In speaking of God, we resort to "anthropomorphism," the application to God of human terminology. Unable to describe God's reality, we use such expressions as God's hand, his face, his anger, his delight - expressions that are theologically inappropriate, yet necessary mental crutches to allow us to speak and think of God. "Father" is merely a metaphor for God's authority and love. In ancient times, all power models were male; so God had to be masculine. The male was the head of the family, of the clan and of the tribe. To evoke God's authority, it was natural, therefore, to use titles such as Father, Lord, or Master. To portray God's might, the Torah even calls him *"Ish Milchama - a warrior."*

The Rabbis of the Talmud were all males. They interpreted Torah with a male bias. They explain, for example, that Aaron, Miriam, and Moses died by "God's kiss," a gentle withdrawal of the soul that God reserves for his favorites. However, in the case of Aaron and Moses the text of the Torah gives us a hint that God kissed them at the moment of death. The Rabbis found no textual indication in the case of Miriam, although God kissed her, too, *"mipnei sheh-g'nai ha-davar l'omro - because it would be embarrassing to mention it"* (Baba Batra 17a). The sages were prepared to concede that God kissed Miriam just as he kissed her brothers, but they were obviously uncomfortable with the idea that such a delicate matter might be reflected in the actual text of the Torah.

The Bible, however, is less self-conscious and freely applies female imagery to God. *"As a man whom his mother comforts, so will I comfort you,"* says God (Isaiah 66:13). In last Shabbat's Torah portion, we read *"Tzur yelad'cha... el m'chol'leka - God gave birth to you ... God writhed in labour with you"* (Deuteronomy

32:18). Here, even the most modern translator in the New Jewish Publication Society Bible loses his nerve: the Hebrew "gave birth" becomes "begat" in English. The translator substitutes the male reproductive function for the female which he is evidently too squeamish to attribute to the Almighty.

One of God's most important ethical attributes is "Rachamim," mercy or compassion. Etymologically it is derived from "rechem - womb," the most female organ. In calling God "merciful" - "baal harachamim" or "ha-rachaman" - we are ascribing to him a very female attribute.

God's presence on earth, his immanence or "in-dwelling," the aspect of the deity that accompanies his people into exile and suffers with them, is called the "Shechina," a feminine term, and often represented symbolically as a woman.

Why is it important, you might ask, how we speak of God? As long as we remember that he is neither male nor female, what do our metaphors matter? Why disturb our comfortable image of God as He, the Man above? After all, only pagans have female deities, goddesses whose worship tends to degenerate to obscenity, while our God is pure and — male!

The first reason is obvious: if we continue to speak of God as male without as much as a disclaimer, we may alienate women.

But there is a more cogent reason: language affects the way we see the world.

Could it not be true, as has been alleged, that using masculine language exclusively to refer to God reinforces a power structure that keeps men in control? Does it not remain easier to justify a social order which denies women equal opportunity, as long as we use only male imagery to describe our God?

Could it just be true, seeing that God is the source of our religious ethic, that our emphasis on his male attributes, the power attributes, has engendered aggressiveness and love of combat? Perhaps an emphasis on his womanly attributes, the giving, caring, pathetic, and empathetic attributes, would ultimately result in an improved human condition?

The most compelling reason to mind our way of talking about God is this: while God is neither male nor female, we all are one or the other. Man or woman, we are expected to make God our role model. We all must find our identity, our personality, grounded

13

in God. Our understanding of God must help us to accept ourselves, to be at peace with ourselves, to be at peace with our own and with the opposite sex. Our idea of God must help us feel comfortable as husbands and wives, sons and daughters, brothers and sisters.

Rabbi Isaac Adarbi, a Jewish philosopher who lived in Salonica, Greece in the 16th Century, poses a very interesting question (Divrei Shalom ch.26): We know that we gain our spiritual perfection through the performance of the Mitzvot, the commandments, which make us fit for life eternal. Jewish Law exempts women from many Mitzvot. How then can women achieve the perfection of their souls? Are they condemned to remain at a lower stage of spiritual growth? Are they disqualified for the highest rungs of eternal blessedness?

Adarbi offers a most surprising answer: women by their very nature are closer to perfection than men, and thus require fewer Mitzvot to become whole and perfect. Male Jews must fulfil all the commandments in order to grow to their full spiritual capacity; women have a head start and reach the same goal with less commandments.

I was surprised by Adarbi's hypothesis. What could be the ground for his bold position?

Pondering this question led me to a fresh discovery in Genesis. Let us look at the account of creation.

Man is created from the dirt, from the earth, *"adama"* in Hebrew and therefore called *"Adam."* Adam means a lump of earth, a clod!

The first female, Eve, was of nobler origin. Created out of Adam, out of the first human being, she was a step removed from the earthy origin of her mate. She was already fashioned out of human material.

In the Biblical creation scheme, woman is thus of a higher order than man.

I was also intrigued by the discovery which I made while looking at the text in Genesis that the Torah does not call Adam *"Ish - Man,"* until the woman is presented to him. Only then does he receive this title: *"le-zot yikarei ishah kee mei'ish lukkacha zot - this one shall be called 'Isha,' a woman, for she was taken from 'ish,' a man"* (Genesis 2:23). Up to this point in the narrative, he was only Adam - the lump of earth! It is the female who endows the Adam-creature with humanity. It is the woman who makes a home out of the cave. It is she who contributes the finer things of life: art, song and music. It is Eve who makes a "mensch" out of the clod!

It cannot be denied that our Jewish tradition supports a role differentiation between male and female. Yet let us try to understand precisely how this differentiation is to be defined.

Women can do practically everything as well as men. They can be equally good, and possibly better, as physicians, lawyers, prime ministers and even rabbis. They are not quite so good as men at things that have to do with "adama," with the earthy, brute part of human endeavour. The fastest female miler is slower than her male counterpart. She cannot, on an average, heave a weight as heavy, nor throw a rock as far as a male.

Women can do what no man ever can: conceive, bear and nourish a baby. While men are indispensable in the process -save for a few reported exceptions in which Jews do not believe- the male function in the process takes only a few minutes. The female role, by contrast, includes not only nine months of gestation but also, at least under more primitive conditions, many more months of nourishing. The Bible calls the first woman "*Chava - Eve*," i.e. she who produces life.

Like it or not, this is at the root of an inescapable male-female differentiation. Man has to wrestle with "Adama;" he is the tiller of the soil, the hunter for the food, the provider and protector. "Adama" is his destiny. The evolution of human society may have made it possible for an individual male to opt out of this role, but broadly and figuratively speaking, the "Earth" may be said to determine the male role.

The same reality compels women in general -excepting again individuals who make alternative choices-to accept responsibility for child-bearing and child-rearing. Theirs is also another major obligation: humanizing the home, the family, and the community.

Our technologically advanced society affords its members a wide range of opportunities beyond the gender-conditioned role. A woman may legitimately choose a working role outside of the home. She has a full right to a career, either in addition to her family role or as an alternative, and she is entitled to full equality in the working world. We should note that Jewish law gives the woman, but not the man, the right to opt out from the duty of procreation.

15

The most important assurance that the Jewish faith offers to both men and women is that they may accept the gender-related part of their role in the confident certainty that in their masculinity and their femininity they relate equally to God.

Let me conclude with a beautiful Talmudic homily!

The Rabbis note the similarity between the Hebrew words for man and woman: "ish" and "isha." The difference is the presence of the letter "Yod" in "ish," and of the letter "Heh" in "isha." These are the two letters which form the sacred name of God. When there is peace between man and woman, the Rabbis say, together they spell God. The difference between male and female is the signature of Divinity! But if there is strife between them, God withdraws his Name and what is left of "ish" and "isha" is "esh, esh," the Hebrew word for "fire."

Let us then pursue harmony between the two halves of humanity and thus put the divine signature on our society. Let us appreciate special responsibilities as partners, rather than adversaries. Let us accord respect and equality to women who choose to exercise their gifts in the competitive world of the market-place. Let us accord respect and equality to women who prefer to concentrate on a role in family and society.

Let us remember that only in mutual love can we spell the name of the One who is neither He nor She, no matter how we speak; who is both Father and Mother, and whom we implore on this day of forgiveness and reconciliation to rise from the *"Kissei Ha-Din - the Throne of Judgement,"* the male throne, and to take a seat on the female throne, the *"Kissei Ha-rachamim - the Throne of Mercy and Compassion."*

Israel: Noun or Verb?

Ecstasy and agony are Israel's gifts to those who love her.

The ecstasy comes from the thrill of knowing that a Jewish State exists. I and many of my contemporaries, who lived through humiliating homelessness, cannot take the Jewish State for granted. It remains miraculous, an incredible salvation. We glory in its achievements, its victories, its beauty.

The agony comes from haunting questions, from nagging doubts, from bitter uncertainties. Alas, there remains a gap between vision and reality which will not be narrowed. There is no peace in the Middle East, and as the years pass by, the prospect of a comprehensive peace remains remote. After peace with Egypt was achieved and Israel declared itself prepared to make peace with its other neighbours, the Palestinians became the stick with which to beat Israel. Even before the "Intifada" erupted, the situation had become ugly. Not only world opinion, but some Israelis and many Jews in the diaspora took a dim view of Israel's response to the Palestinian problem. A few Jews outside Israel voiced criticism publicly; most preferred to be discreet.

"Love without criticism is no love!" the Sages say. When Israel was the subject of my sermons, I would often enter a passionate plea for Israel's vindication and try to show the unfairness of most of Israel's critics. But loving Israel, I could not always withhold criticism myself.

My Independence Day Sermon in 1987, another difficult year for Israel and her loving supporters, exemplified my ecstasy and my agony, my impatience with the gap between vision and reality, and most of all, my love.

Israel: Noun or Verb?—————————————
A sermon for Israel's Independence Day - Yom Ha'atzma'ut preached on Parshat Tazri'a-Metzora 1987 - 5747

Last week, the Torah portion contained the dietary rules, the laws concerning clean and unclean animals. The Sages call this chapter *"Torat B'hema - the Law of the Beast."* Today's Torah reading includes the chapter which they call *"Torat Adam - the Torah of Man,"* a section dealing with clean and unclean conditions that apply to human beings.

The Talmud offers a rationale for the sequence of the chapters which puts the animals first, the human beings last.

> *Said Rabbi Simla'i: "Just as in the Order of Creation the origin of Man came after the origin of the animals, so the Torah of Man is presented after the Torah of the Beast"* (Midrash Rabba Vayikra 14:1).

The order of creation, in the rabbinic view, puts the human being into an ambivalent position. He was created last because he is the crown of creation, the culmination of evolution. The origin of all other creatures was but preamble to the appearance of the human species. However, if humans fail to appreciate their excellence implicit in the order of creation, if they do not live up to the human potential and commitment, they may be put in their place by a curt reminder: *"Yattush k'damcha - the insects even came before you!"* (ibid). You are a late arrival on the scene. You have no cause for conceit! Be humble therefore!

This coming Monday we observe a great festival. It is "Yom Ha-atzma'ut - Israel Independence Day." Many of us are too young to remember the events that brought Israel into being, but others will never forget the birth of the Jewish State.

The United Nations had approved the creation of a Jewish State in a partitioned Palestine. The Jews had accepted the plan; the Arabs rejected it. Britain had announced its firm intention to terminate its mandate over Palestine on May 14, 1948 - the fifth of Iyyar in the Jewish calendar. Weeks before, the British initiated the gradual evacuation of their forces to their naval base in Haifa. In the process, they handed over many military strong points and strategic positions to Arab forces, while disarming the Jewish population.

All over the country, Arabs went on the attack against the Jews. Many Jewish settlements were isolated and came under siege. From across the Jordan, Arab "volunteers," not answerable to any Arab government, reinforced the local Arab combatants and formed an army of irregulars. Meanwhile, the regular armies of Egypt, Syria, Transjordan and Lebanon, with contingents from other Arab States, massed on the borders of Palestine, waiting for the official end of the British mandate. Then they would swoop down on the mere six hundred thousand Jews of Palestine and, it was expected, make short shrift of them.

Around the world, a frantic diplomatic initiative was launched to convince Britain to stay longer and to persuade the Jews to delay their proclamation of independence. Their plight was hopeless, Jews were told. The survival of a Jewish state under present conditions would be impossible; their proposed step would be suicidal.

But the Jews of Palestine knew their hour of destiny was at hand. They had waited long enough. The Jewish people had waited for two thousand years, through centuries of persecution, through the hell of a Holocaust.

Their dream was not to be denied. There was no turning back now.

The eyes of the world were upon them - and the eyes of generations past, of martyrs, of victims.

The rest is history. David Ben-Gurion read the Proclamation of Independence. The impossible became reality. Supplies and munitions began to flow to a beleaguered Jewish population. Arab armies were routed in a painful, costly struggle for survival.

Israel is now thirty-nine years old.

On the gauge of history, Israel is still a newcomer, a young nation. It arrived centuries after such states as Spain, Portugal, France, and Britain. Thus, born last, it might represent the culmination of history, just as the arrival of the first human being represented the culmination of creation. The proviso remains, however, that Israel must exemplify "Torat Adam," the Torah of Humanity, not "Torat B'hema," the Law of the Jungle.

Has Israel lived up to its promise?

We expected Israelis to build a model society. The Declaration of Independence contained promises that sketched an ideal community.

19

It was to be based on equality and justice, on prosperity created by science and industry, on peace achieved by cooperation. The Declaration anticipated the fulfilment of Messianic tasks, such as the ingathering of the exiles. We looked forward to a central fountainhead of Jewish spirituality for all corners of the Jewish world.

We must record, regretfully, some disappointments.

Israel has made its mistakes. Like other countries of the world, Israel has been singed by scandals and corruption. Israel has not yet grown entirely out of the stages of "Torat B'hema." When one of its economically most significant exports has to be the trade in weapons, when the need to survive mandates arms deals even with a country such as Iran, we know that Israel has a long way yet to go before it will arrive at its promised destination.

The observer of the Israeli scene may note with concern that the growth of prosperity has been accompanied, just as elsewhere, by a growth of materialism. We are uncomfortable with the spectacle of social strife fuelled by the unequal distribution of wealth. We are disheartened by Israel's religious divisiveness, even though it is benign compared to religious conflicts in other parts of the world.

Above all, we are discouraged by the lack of progress in the search for peace. We feel frustrated by the futility of meeting terrorism with countermeasures that appear to escalate the levels of violence without providing a remedy.

Yet on the other side of the ledger, there is much cause for happiness.

A short while ago, on Holocaust Remembrance Day, I spoke to an assembly of Jewish school children. How can you explain the horror of the Holocaust to children without frightening them about the future? I had the answer. "There was no State of Israel in existence at that time to protect Jews and to offer them refuge."

Israel's record of Ingathering the Exiles, or to put it in less Messianic terms, its refugee policy, is unprecedented in its generosity. The absorption of immigrants in numbers exceeding its population at the time is an abidingly glorious achievement. The merit of this policy easily outweighs all the negatives that may be adduced by Israel's detractors.

Israel has achieved miracles in agronomy. Its agricultural science and technology will turn out to be the blessing of the Middle East, whenever peace may be established. Its universities and other scientific institutions have scored great success in medicine and various scientific and technological enterprises which boost our pride and confidence in Israel's future.

Let us not forget that Israel is and remains the only true democracy in the Middle East. For a small country labouring since its inception under wartime conditions, a thriving democratic system is no mean achievement.

Thirty-nine years ago, when the Jewish state was about to be born, people were trying to guess what the new country's name was going to be. It had been kept secret. Would it be called "Zion" after Zionism? Would the name be "Judah," reviving the name of the last state we had?

The Declaration of Independence disclosed that the name was to be Israel. It was the name our ancestor Jacob had received because he had *"wrestled with the divine and with the human"* (Genesis 32:29). That struggle, between a human reality and a divine calling, is the challenge of our Jewish state today and, it seems, for some time yet to come.

The name "Israel" is really a verb, not a noun. Grammatically, it is the imperfect form of the verb, indicating incompleteness or ongoing action. Rather than name a completed accomplishment, it hints at continuing progress. "Israel" means *"he will continue to wrestle;"* the struggle goes on.

On this Yom Ha-atzma'ut, we shall proclaim our faith in the future of Israel. Israel will proceed from "Torat B'hema" to "Torat Adam." It will raise the level of what may be expected of human beings. It will demonstrate the capability of humanity at its best. Last week, on Holocaust Remembrance Day, we shuddered remembering how deep the Human Being can sink into the "Torat B'hema," the abyss of his animal nature. On Yom Ha-Atzma'ut, the joy of the festival will give us a glimpse of heights yet unscaled to which we pray Israel will rise in its quest for the "Torah of Man."

For this quest we pledge our support, our faith, our loyalty and love.

Fools, Criminals or Heroes?

Direct political action was spawned in the turbulence of North American society in the '50s. Out of the sit-ins and protest marches that marked the Civil Rights struggle in the United States, there developed a tactic designed to short-cut the processes for achieving social change. Conventional means of reforming society and modifying the legal system were too slow and circuitous. Direct action, dramatic, drastic, attention-getting and photogenic, promised more immediate results. Direct action provided also an outlet for justified impatience and genuine desperation.

This new form of radical political activism disdained legal norms. It disregarded private or government property and ignored good manners and civility. Direct action has been ever since a feature of our political life. Students have occupied university offices and sometimes trashed expensive lab equipment. Pacifists have invaded military bases and industrial plants. To this day, anti-abortionists try to prevent abortions by physically barring access to clinics.

Is direct action morally justifiable?

In 1975, Dr. Henry Morgenthaler made news with illegal abortion clinics. An activist in the cause of more liberal access to abortion for the women of Canada, he was repeatedly arrested, charged with illegal operation of abortion clinics and occasionally jailed. However, he was acquitted in an important precedent-setting jury trial. It was shortly after that trial that I utilized the Biblical account of the zealot Pinchas to discuss the problem of direct political action in a sermon.

Neither in Canada nor in other parts of the world did direct political action go out of fashion.

In 1985, I was invited to write a Rabbinic comment on the portion of Pinchas for the "Wochenblatt," the weekly newspaper of the Jewish congregations in Germany. Shortly before, Jews in Frankfurt had physically prevented the production of a play they deemed to be anti-Semitic by occupying the stage. Therefore a discussion of zealotry and direct political action was very topical.

My article in the "Wochenblatt" became the basis for a new sermon on the subject when the Torah portion of Pinchas was read in 1986.

Fools, Criminals or Heroes?
A Sermon Preached on Parshat Pinchas 5746 - 1986

In modern Hebrew, the word *"Kanna'i"* denotes a "fanatic, extremist." It is often used in a disparaging sense. Earlier in our history, the term *"Kanna'im"* described the "Zealots" who instigated uprisings against the Roman authorities and who achieved immortality in their fanatical defense of Massada.

In the Bible, where the word originates, its root is eminently respectable. Its meaning is "to be zealous, to act with zeal." The Lord Himself is introduced as *"El Kanna - the Zealous God."*

This word is also the key word in the tribute to Pinchas which opens the Torah portion named after this hero. He achieved immortal fame when he took decisive direct action at a time of national emergency. The Israelites were about to squander the momentum of their progress to the Promised Land in a large-scale outbreak of idolatrous sexual orgies with the *"Daughters of Moab"* leading to the total demoralization of the people. At this crucial moment, Pinchas rose up in the midst of a confused and helpless assembly of the elders, took a spear and killed Zimri, an Israelite noble, together with his socially prominent Moabite partner, *in flagrante delicto,* thus halting a plague which God had inflicted on the people for their debauchery.

God himself praised Pinchas' zealous act:

> *Pinchas the son of Eleazar, the son of Aaron the Priest, has turned aside my anger from the people of Israel when he displayed his zeal on my behalf (b'kann'o et kinn'ati) in their midst, so that I did not finish off the people of Israel in my zealousness (b'kinn'ati). Therefore say to him, "Behold, I offer him my covenant of peace...because he acted zealously (kinnei) for his God"* (Bamidbar 25:11-13).

23

Passion and zeal are evidently praiseworthy in a right cause. Bold, decisive, direct action, receives God's approval.

It comes as a surprise therefore that the teachers of our Jewish tradition had serious reservations. It appears that they could not condone a person taking the law into his own hands, no matter how sincere his motives.

The Talmudic teachers subtly put the critique of Pinchas' action into the mouth of his contemporary sages.

> *Pinchas acted contrary to the will of the Sages; they would have excommunicated him if the Holy Spirit had not preempted their move and proclaimed "Behold, I offer him my covenant of peace"* (Talmud Yerushalmi Sanhedrin 9:7).

The conflict of values revealed in this Talmudic passage has never been more topical than at this time. The contradictory points-of-view are the subject of present-day controversies that affect us deeply. How are we to view zealotry, i.e. unilateral direct extremist action in the service of a higher "right?" Does the justice of the ultimate cause excuse the breaking of laws deemed to be irrelevant or insignificant in relation to the moral purpose?

The Talmudic passage implying criticism of Pinchas strongly suggests that there is a moral ambivalence. On the one hand, there is a "human perspective" represented by the sages who opposed Pinchas. On the other hand, there is a "divine perspective," God's own response which vindicates and applauds Pinchas. How can we be sure in any given case that what we hear is the voice of "the Holy Spirit" and not the voice of self-righteous fanaticism?

Zealotry of varying degrees is very much in evidence today. People are driven to direct extra-legal action by the force of their convictions. A higher justice, many of them claim, hallows their illegal means. Jewish settlers in Judah and Samaria form vigilante squads; anti-abortionists invade private property to stop what they call murder; activist rabbis and other clergy defy the law to demonstrate at Soviet embassies; anti-nuclear protesters either surround army bases to prevent the installation of missiles, or interfere with the production of arms; indignant citizens stop the performance of a blatantly offensive play by occupying the stage.

May one take the law into his own hands in the face of official or public lethargy? Is Pinchas a hero, or a misguided, even criminal fool?

24

Clearly, the Sages of the Talmud take a dim view of the *"kanna'i,"* the zealot who is his own judge and jury. They are suspicious of charismatic heroes and their motivations which, they claim, place them above the law. The Sages recommend that we pursue our objectives within legal parameters, by just means. The end does not hallow all means.

Yet the Sages are also compelled to admit that there are exceptional cases, in which the law may be overruled.

We must be open to the possibility of circumstances that call for direct, decisive, bold action, regardless of what the law allows. Righteous indignation does exist. The hero must take a chance; he cannot help it. He must stake his honour, his place in society, his very life on his being right. He must accept the risk of being judged presumptuous and be prepared to suffer the consequences. He can never be sure, for the "Holy Spirit" may remain silent. Yet if he refuses to take that risk, he may miss his star hour, his appointment with destiny, his call to greatness. Only his own inner resources can guide him. And only his contemporaries – or posterity– will judge whether he was deluded in his conceit or whether he was one of the chosen few whom the "Holy Spirit" vindicates and, in return for daring infamy and death, offers the everlasting "Covenant of Peace."

25

Emotions on Demand

Reason and emotion are the twin guides of human conduct. Very often, they send us contradictory signals: our head would have us do one thing, our heart another. How we decide may reflect our basic personality or temperament. Some of us are inclined to act by reason, others by feeling. Yet our moods are not constant, regardless of any existing predisposition. Our decision-making, therefore, may be inconsistent.

The spirit of the time affects our decision-making as well. Societies are subject to epochal changes. We speak of the Romantic Age, the Age of Enlightenment and other identifiable epochs in cultural history. These are long-term modulations of the civilizational climate. But in the collective psyche of a society, there are also quickly fluctuating short-term trends that change almost with the speed of fashion. Psychologists, sociologists, historians, philosophers, and other observers of the scene enjoy analyzing these trends, defining them customarily in units of decades: the sixties, the seventies and so forth.

It seems to me that the outcome of the contest between reason and emotion has been increasingly tilting toward the emotional side of the spectrum. "If it feels right, do it!" says our modern wisdom. "Do you feel comfortable with it?" is the crucial question to ascertain whether a certain course of action is appropriate. Feeling, rather than rational thought, is the dominant factor in decision-making and is accepted as proper by most of those who judge our behaviour.

As rabbi, I must be a judge and critic of what people do. My standards must be objective and more absolute than the gauge of personal feeling and emotional comfortableness.

On a summer visit to Israel, I was struck by the emotion displayed by some pious people observing Tish'a B'Av, the day of national mourning for the destruction of Jerusalem and the Holy Temple two thousand years ago. The sun is shining on the rebuilt Jerusalem, a city beautiful and crowded with happy throngs of busy people, a thriving metropolis, capital of a flourishing State of Israel. Yet mourners are sitting on the ground, swaying back and forth in obvious despair and grief uttering tearful lamentations as if the calamity had just happened yesterday and Jerusalem lay in ashes, God forbid!

It was then that I decided to prepare a sermon on "Emotions on Demand."

Emotions on Demand
Preached on Parshat Kee Tavo 5746 - 1986

Emotions are the music of life. Life would be drab and monotonous without joy and sadness, love and hate, sympathy, envy, pride, fear, hope or despair. The rainbow spectrum of human feelings gives our lives texture and colour. Take away emotion and we would be mere robots mechanically performing our tasks.

It is normal and healthy to feel strongly. Absence of emotional response is often indicative of personality disorders.

Judaism, therefore, has a great deal to say about feelings. The inclusive, embracing emotions that make us reach out, such as joy, love and pity, are generally held to be good. Others, generally the exclusive feelings that tend to insulate us, are considered bad. Among these are anger, envy and pride.

It is remarkable, though, that Judaism, not satisfied with merely grading emotions, dares to regulate them. On Tish'a B'Av, the ninth of Av, the recently observed anniversary of the destruction of the Temple and the burning of Jerusalem, we were expected to feel sorrow and anguish and to become mourners. Every Shabbat since that date, we have been reading the Haftaras of Consolation. These are the chapters of comfort from the Book of Isaiah in which the prophet exults in the certainty of the coming redemption and raises the hopes of the despairing nation. Listening today to the sixth Haftara of the series, we are to take heart. "Arise, shine, for your light has come!" Mourn no longer, be comforted, lift your depressed spirits!

How can we be expected to feel emotion on demand? Is it not absurd to ask us to experience genuine sorrow and comfort according to the calendar? Feelings are feelings. They are spontaneous, involuntary, beyond our control. You do not plan to have feelings. You do not decide, "Today I'm going to be sad; this afternoon I'm going to feel compassionate; tonight I'm going to be nostalgic." You wake up one morning and feel lousy, depressed —and don't worry if you do. It's normal. Another morning may find you in an upbeat mood, feeling just "great!"

Feelings often depend on what happens to you. How you feel has nothing to do with your volition; you cannot help it. You have an unpleasant encounter and your mood changes. A person experiences a misfortune and the natural reaction is sadness and grief. The Toronto Blue Jays lose again, and you feel anger, frustration and disgust. Emotions are involuntary reactions to reality.

Judaism seems to disagree. It downgrades the spontaneous, involuntary nature of emotion and commands us to emote certain ways at certain times. On the High Holy Days and before, we are to experience awe and fear. On Sukkot, we are to feel joy and gratitude, even if we had no special reason to be joyful or grateful. "You must rejoice," the Torah commands so many times. When the month of Adar begins two weeks before Purim, the Shulchan Aruch enjoins that we must feel a heightened sense of joy: *"marbim b'simcha."* During the so-called "Three Weeks" we are supposed to feel sad. In some old prayerbooks with Yiddish annotations intended mainly for the women folk, you come across a page where an instruction reads *"Do veint men! - Here you weep."* And even if the women did not understand the text of the prayer they were reading, they cried and shed real tears.

A death occurs, God forbid. Jewish law decrees deep mourning, the Shiv'a, so severe in its rules that few nowadays observe it strictly without compromise. Yet, no matter how tragic the loss and how deep the feeling of sorrow, when the Shiv'a is over you must accept comfort. You must open your heart to consolation and eventually to healing. Sometimes a Shiv'a is terminated prematurely by the onset of a festival; while your fellow Jews are rejoicing, you must not surrender to your private sorrow. In the most extreme case, when a burial takes place in the midst of a week-long festival, you are expected to suspend your grief, in order to join your fellow Jews in the festive period. Only when the festival is over, you sit down and mourn! Is that not indeed absurd?

Judaism expects you to manage your emotions! You can exercise a degree of control over them, and you must!

It is not demanded of you to suppress emotions; on the contrary, that would be unhealthy and wrong. But no matter how genuine and strong a feeling may be, it is not a run-away horse; you can curb, guide and direct it! You must treat your feeling with respect; you are to give it a little free rein and accommodate it to a degree, but then you must pull in the reins and exercise a degree of control. You must manage your feelings!

Emotions are essentially unstable. Like unstable substances, they deteriorate and change into something else. Contentment is a commendable feeling, but indulge it too much, and it may turn into smugness. If such positive emotions as joy and happiness are not managed, they may change to self-love, narcissism and insular insensitivity for others. Similarly, if sadness and sorrow are not managed, they will turn into depression and spiritual paralysis.

Judaism gives you prescriptions for the management of emotion. You must direct it into proper channels, and thus stabilize the emotion, or help it evolve creatively. In happiness you are not to yield to selfish euphoria. You are reminded that such joy will not last; sharing your good fortune with others is part of the prescription. Again and again, the Torah joins the command to be joyful with taking responsibility for the "Levite, the stranger, the widow and the orphan." An example is found in today's Torah portion, where the joy of the first-fruit offering is to be expressed by sharing with the less privileged.

In grief, look for sources of comfort and open your heart to those who try to comfort you. Believe the truth that pain, even the most severe, will ultimately pass. Do not feel guilty when pain diminishes and thus retard its passing. When you love, feel love deeply and exult in it, but know that love must lead to responsibility, for otherwise it will deteriorate. Be angry if you cannot avoid it, but know that anger cannot last forever, that it must yield in due course to appeasement and reconciliation. Hate if you must -we are allowed, even commanded, to hate evil, though not the evildoer- but you must attenuate hatred, modifying it with reason so that it will spur you to work for the removal of the evil you hate.

Follow the path of Jewish living which leads you through a veritable garden of emotional variety. Experience the highs and the lows of the calendar; feel the joys and the sorrows of the community. Rejoice in the festivals, each with its own nuance of joy and meaning. When you welcome the Shabbat with Kiddush, yield to its serenity

29

and contentment and celebrate what you have achieved in the six days of labour. On Shabbat, you make peace with the world as it is. And when you take leave again of Shabbat with Havdala and its flickering fire -the means and the symbol of man's conquest of the environment- feel again the creative discontent with things as they are. That feeling urges you to try to make the world into what it should be. God is waiting for you to finish His creation. And realize that you yourself are not finished yet, but do not allow this self-critical sense to turn to despondency; rather let it goad you towards greater perfection. And thank God for impatience and frustration as you thank him for happiness and peace.

Questions for Conservative Jews

Adath Israel Congregation joined the Conservative Movement and affiliated with the United Synagogue of America in 1956. It was a time when the Jewish community of Toronto was shifting to the suburbs and many new Synagogues were being built.

Almost by intuition, Synagogue leaders knew that the orientation of Conservative Judaism and its practices were just right for their congregations, even though its ideology was but imperfectly understood. Somehow, Conservative Judaism seemed to offer a comfortable compromise between Orthodoxy and Reform.

My Passover sermon in 1964 was part of a program to teach what Conservative Judaism really meant. A better understanding of our movement would lead, and eventually did lead, to a more serious commitment to Jewish observance.

A few weeks earlier, on March 22, 1964, Dr. Simon Greenberg, Vice-Chancellor of the Jewish Theological Seminary, was the main speaker at a Day of Study for Conservative Synagogue leaders in Toronto. The discussion which took place on that occasion suggested to me the theme of my sermon. For some of its ideas I am indebted to Dr. Greenberg.

Questions for Conservative Jews ———————
Preached on Passover 5724 - 1964

Suddenly without explanation, so the story goes, the Rabbi, a fine young man, resigned from his position. The perplexed congregation, hastily assembled, sent the President to ascertain the reason for the Rabbi's mystifying decision.

"Why, dear Rabbi, would you want to leave our wonderful congregation?" Said the Rabbi: "Because in my three years in this community this is the first question anyone ever asked me!"

A Rabbi wants to be asked. A question directed to him has a special term in the vocabulary of Jewish life: a "Shaaleh" or to use the precise Hebrew form, "Sh'eilah." To "pasken a Shaaleh" - to give an authoritative decision in a question of Jewish Law - has always been the Rabbi's primary function; it is for this that he was really ordained. Any knowledgeable person can preach a sermon or deliver a lecture, but only the ordained Rabbi can decide a case of legal doubt and declare an act or thing allowed or forbidden, kosher or trefa, right or wrong, true or false.

An entire branch of Rabbinic literature, called "Sh'eilot u-T'shuvot," literally "Questions and Answers," preserves the learned opinions and decisions which Rabbinic authorities have rendered over many centuries. This "Responsa Literature," as it is modernly called, comprises well over a thousand volumes of dissertations written in reply to the practical questions submitted by communities or rabbis, the questions themselves often consisting of learned arguments and hypotheses to be evaluated and decided upon by the rabbi to whom they were addressed.

Not only are these books important to the student of Jewish jurisprudence, but they are a mine of valuable information and source material for the historian, because, as the questions relate to actual practical problems, they reflect the changing conditions of Jewish life. They mirror the crises of sorely exploited medieval Jewish communities, right down to the agonies of Nazi extermination camps whose inmates asked the rabbi in their midst whether a woman may use contraceptives, since pregnancy usually meant prompt dispatch to the gas chamber.

Notwithstanding their general importance in Jewish life, all questions are not of the same degree of pertinence and quality. The Pessach Haggadah, which in a strict sense is one long answer to the "Four Questions" at the Seder's beginning, distinguishes between different classes of questions: *"Echad Chacham, echad Rasha, echad Tam..."* the questions, respectively, of *"the wise son, the wicked and the simple one."*

But it is not the intrinsic quality of the question alone that determines to which category it belongs. The personality, intent and attitude of the questioner is just as significant in evaluating a question as its substance and phraseology. There is not too much difference, on the surface, between the question of the Chacham, the Wise, and of the Rasha, the Wicked. The former's question is wise because it aims at deepening and widening knowledge; the latter's question is wicked because it is meant to express scorn and personal aloofness. The identity of the questioner and his intent, as much as what he asks, determines how good a question is.

Whenever Conservative Judaism is seriously discussed, one specific charge is usually levelled against it: Conservative Judaism refuses to give clear and definite answers to questions. Whatever guidance it offers is alleged to be vague and evasive.

"We want clear answers! Spell out for us definitively what we may do, as Conservative Jews, and what not! Tell us yes or no! Give us a code, a new Conservative Shulchan Aruch! Give us a guide for Jewish conduct in precisely defined terms! Clarify our ideology; state our theology; tell us what we must believe!"

Are these the questions of the Tam, the simple one, who wants direction, or the questions of the Chacham, the Wise, who wants to pursue his quest for knowledge and for more meaningful Jewish living? Or might some of these questions come from the Rasha, the Wicked one, who asks not to end confusion but in order to confuse; who ridicules in order to avoid personal involvement and to find an alibi for his indifference.

Let me give you a few examples. One question I am often asked concerns "non-kosher" wine. "May I, a member of a Conservative Synagogue, drink non-Jewish wine? I know the Orthodox prohibit it; for the Reform Jew there is no problem - but what is our position?"

Is it a good question? Well, it depends. If, for example, a generally observant person would like to indulge his taste for wine, the question is perfectly legitimate. More often, however, I have been asked this question by individuals who do not observe Kashrut, even in its most elementary form. Why would such individuals worry about kosher wine?

It recalls the story of the man who was so pious that he boasted of three sets of dentures. "Why do you need three?" he was asked. "One for meat and one for dairy," was the reply. "Alright; but why the third?" "Well, sometimes I like to eat a little piece of ham."

Favourite questions are those relating to the Sabbath. "May we

33

switch on electric lights? Am I allowed to drive to Shule? Why can I not play golf on Shabbat afternoon?"

The questioner does not know, of course, that many of these questions have been asked and answered many times over. Many Conservative Synagogues offer an extensive program of adult education, and problems of Jewish law are usually given serious attention. No matter how many the lectures on Conservative Judaism, most of the people who complain about its vagueness can rarely be found in attendance. Aloof and supercilious, they cannot be bothered, except that they dare you to "try and answer this one" to their satisfaction at their convenience, without much relevance to their personal conduct, actual or intended.

Many modern questions have been dealt with by the Law Committee of the Conservative Rabbinate. In a formal responsum, after the manner of the classical "T'shuvah," the Rabbinical Assembly has under certain conditions permitted travel to the Synagogue on the Sabbath. Now, for whom is this T'shuvah intended? It is intended for the Sabbath observer; for the person who makes a serious and sincere effort to observe the Sabbath in a meaningful way, but cannot walk to the Synagogue. It is entirely irrelevant, however, to the person who ignores the observance of the Sabbath. If he does not feel he needs an excuse, and indeed has none, for working, shopping, travelling, gardening, house cleaning, car washing, on the Sabbath; if his home knows no candles, no Kiddush, no Shabbat atmosphere; if his automobile takes him to many places and activities in flagrant conflict with the spirit and the tradition of the Shabbat, why should driving to the Synagogue weigh so heavily on his conscience that he must ask the Rabbi, especially since he has little intention of going to services in the first place. Such questions, I am afraid, belong to the "Rasha" category. They are but mockery and hypocrisy.

Conservative Judaism is not ambiguous at all as to the broad areas of required observance. No one who has ever attended a lecture, read a book, an article, or even listened to a few sermons on the subject can sincerely charge Conservative Judaism with being vague about the duties of a Jew. As the prophet said, *"Higgid lecha adam ma tov - you have been told, o man, what is good and what the Lord demands of you"* (Micha 6:8).

Conservative Judaism demands of the Jew full compliance with the ethical principles and practices of our tradition and law. It insists, for example, on scrupulous honesty and fairness in our business dealings; it expects us to be alert to justice in our private lives as well as in our community; it challenges us to develop a moral character and a sense of responsibility toward family and society.

Conservative Judaism demands compliance with the ritual practices of our law and tradition, which it claims cannot be divorced from the domain of ethics. Conservative Judaism unequivocally stresses the observance of Shabbat to the fullest extent of the individual's ability. This includes abstaining from work, even at a sacrifice, refraining from travelling and from forms of recreation incompatible with the atmosphere of the Sabbath; and on the positive side, the hallowing of the Sabbath by means of candles, Kiddush, family fellowship, and prayer at the Synagogue. In this sphere, as in others, there is neither hesitation nor ambiguity. Quite to the contrary, there is ample scope for practically everyone to improve his Sabbath observance before he reaches the peripheral borderland where there might be some area of doubt or where the delineation of the Conservative imperative might appear uncertain.

The centrality and importance of the Synagogue is another essential principle in the life of a Conservative Jew, not only in terms of membership and financial support but in terms of participation and attendance for prayer and study. In fact, it is only because congregational worship is so important that the prohibition of travelling on the Sabbath was relaxed, not because the restrictions which insure the sanctity of the Sabbath were deemed obsolete, superfluous or too strict. Yet few of those who profess to be so disturbed by the marginal problems of Conservative Judaism step on the central plank of its platform: personal attendance at Synagogue.

Conservative Judaism urges absolute adherence to Kashruth, both at home and away from it. True, the Conservative interpretation of Jewish law condones the eating of fish, eggs, or similar Kosher foods at non-kosher restaurants when circumstances necessitate it, but no one can sincerely doubt our commitment to Kashruth. It would be sheer hypocrisy to argue about any leniencies as long as we disregard the more basic rules of Kashruth in our personal conduct.

Why should we quibble about commas, semi-colons and periods when we have not even read the paragraph yet? How can anyone expect to be taken seriously if he raises questions about minor details before he has committed himself to the observance of major fundamentals?

35

First we must be prepared to make an honest effort to accept the obligation of Mitzvot in the wide areas of life in which we may serve God and plant the seeds of holiness; afterwards we may then inquire how we should till the less accessible furrows near the limits of our reach. Then we shall ask: May I or may I not? Must I or am I excused?

Take questions of belief and faith.

Is the Torah really the word of God according to Conservative Judaism? Is there an afterlife? We know the Orthodox position; we know the Reform attitude; but what is Conservative philosophy?

Can one brief answer to such complicated questions change your own beliefs in the twinkle of an eye? Can I in one sentence, in one minute, condense the dialogue of generations? There is only one answer: study the Torah! This is another basic requirement of the Conservative Movement. True to the spirit of Jewish tradition, we give top priority to the study of Torah. Not only a maximal Jewish education for our children, but the pursuit of Jewish learning by every Jewish man and woman is an imperative of the Conservative Movement.

Go and study! This is the proper reply to questions of theology so often raised by those who never open a book, nor listen to a lecture. Go and study! Then you may learn the teachings of Judaism and the truths discovered by our thinkers and sages, including the meaning of Torah as the word of God.

Who are the people who ask for a new Conservative Shulchan Aruch? Do they want a new code so as to govern themselves more meaningfully according to God's commandments and to enhance their standards of observance? No. Most people who ask for a new Shulchan Aruch are looking for an official stamp of approval on their standards of non-observance and for an endorsement of their indifference.

The Conservative position is clear. You must do your own personal best to live up to your responsibilities as a Jew. You must make a genuine effort.

As long as a person honestly tries his best to live a Jewish life, even if he should fall short of our standards because of economic, social or educational handicaps, we shall not minimize his worth or deny him first-class citizenship in our religious community. We shall not deprive him of the privilege of being called to the Torah or of participating in every aspect of our religious life. As long as he does his best, he is second to none. But we shall never concede that the best he can do under his particular circumstances should be the norm for all and that no one need do more.

We neither expect everyone to achieve the absolute maximum, nor are we prepared to accept the minimum as the universal standard. What Conservative Judaism demands is a truly serious effort, a constant striving for improvement and for higher levels of Jewish achievement, and a gradual ascent, rung by rung, toward the summit of faith.

By all means, let us continue to ask questions. Let us also remember that the Hebrew word "Teshuvah" does not mean "Answer" only, but also "Return" and "Repentance." So let our questions be those of the Chacham: serious, perceptive, respectful, and intelligent questions; questions relevant to our own commitment, born out of understanding, leading to further knowledge and deeper insight and turning us back "in complete repentance" to the true course of Jewish life.

When More is not Enough

After an initial period of recession, the 1980's were a time of great prosperity. North Americans discovered the "good" life. Standards of living rose. Incomes climbed. Real estate boomed.

It was a time for buying things: computers, VCRs, portable phones -gadgets of every description. It was a time of conspicuous consumption.

Luxury homes were in great demand. Chalets in the ski country and condos in the southern resorts were part of the life style.

The pursuit of pleasure enthralled more and more people.

In the corporate world, greed was the key word. Junk bonds and leveraged buy-outs made bizarre corporate acquisitions possible. Giant conglomerates proliferated and tried to devour one another.

It was a time of hedonism and materialism.

Materialism and hedonism are inimical to Jewish values. Unbridled pursuit of pleasure and profit stifles spirituality. On a practical level, it is difficult, if not impossible, to reconcile living with the profit-and-pleasure principle and the sacrifices that Jewish living demands, except perhaps in the area of conspicuous philanthropy.

It was a problem I addressed repeatedly in the course of those years. The sermon I preached on Rosh Hashana 1987 is an example.

Strange: one of my thoughtful and faithful listeners, remembering this sermon a few years later, referred to it as a sermon about "family." He was right. Though I did not say it explicitly, the spirit and the life style of the 1980's put great strain on the fabric of the Jewish family. The suggestions I made to my congregants are certainly conducive to a better family life.

When More is not Enough ─────────────
A Sermon preached on Rosh Hashana 5748 - 1987

The film "OLIVER!" pictures a poignant scene which Charles Dickens created in his novel "Oliver Twist."

It is supper time in the orphanage. Little Oliver, timid but emboldened by starvation, does the unthinkable.

"Please, Sir; may I have some more?"

"What?" bellows the incredulous warden, who has been ladling out meagre portions of thin gruel into the bowls of the hungry orphans.

"What?" he thunders again, shocked and outraged at the provocative temerity of the hungry child.

"Oliver wants more!" replies the chorus of the orphan boys.

Like Oliver, we too stand, bowl in hand, before the feeding trough of life.

"I want more! I am not satisfied yet! I am still hungry!"

No matter how much we have, we try to get more. To get more is the purpose for which we are working most of the time. We want a higher income, a better return on our investment, a bigger house, a finer car and a longer boat.

Oliver wants more!

To want more is not necessarily wrong. Oliver was entitled to more. He should have had enough to eat.

According to Talmudic moral psychology, we are motivated by two opposite drives or inclinations. We have a *"Yetzer Hatov"* and a *"Yetzer Hara,"* a good and an evil inclination. Of course, we are to obey the counsel of the good inclination, but even the evil inclination, the Yetzer Hara, has its proper place in the scheme of things. If it were not for the prodding of the Yetzer Hara, the ancient sages observe, human beings would neither till the soil, nor do business, nor procreate. They would lack the incentive, the self-interest, the profit motive or the sexual desire. Without these manifestations of the evil inclination we could not maintain the human enterprise. Civilization, and humanity itself, would quickly disappear.

39

If Stone Age people had not wanted more, they would have remained nomads and food gatherers rather than become farmers; hunters rather than domesticators of animals; cave dwellers rather than house builders.

Without wanting more, there is no progress.

The religions of the Far East, in contrast to Bible-based Judaism and Christianity, stress the virtue of not wanting. Want nothing, they say, and you will be spared the unhappiness of inevitable frustration and disappointment. It is interesting to note that while adherents of these religions have attained remarkable heights of spirituality, the societies most influenced by them have lagged behind Western nations in terms of technology and science.

They lacked the incentive of "wanting more."

What is wrong, then, with our wanting more?

The trouble is, our appetite is insatiable. We never have enough. Oliver knew why he wanted more. He was still hungry. We want more even when we are full. A greedy, voracious craving does not let us stop.

"A lover of money never has his fill of money," we read in the Book of Ecclesiastes (5:9). Our Sages observe, *"If a person has a hundred pieces of silver, he wants two hundred."*

Greed is not limited to individuals. Today, we witness also corporate greed. Companies are on the prowl for ever more other companies to swallow. Top executives are driven to enlarge their corporate structures and to build colossal empires.

Another error is that we misinterpret our hunger.

Why is it that when we have doubled our income, it still does not seem enough? Why after we moved into the bigger house, have we still not found the Shangri-La we were seeking?

It is because we mistakenly assume that our lack of contentment with the things we have is a craving for more of the same.

The truth is that we are hungry for another dimension in life.

There was once a family, so the story goes, so poor that they did not have enough to eat. One day, the woman found two coins. She gave them to her husband and asked him to go out and buy their necessities. He bought bread with one coin; a rose with the other.

The wife turned to him puzzled. "Why did we need a rose?"

Said he: "We needed the bread to sustain life. We needed the rose to make life worth living."

We mistakenly believe that we crave the second loaf of bread. The truth is we crave the rose.

Said the prophet Amos:

> "Behold there are days to come," is the oracle of the Lord,
> "when I will send famine into the land; not a famine
> for bread, and neither thirst for water, but to hear the
> words of the Lord" (Amos 8:11).

Our hunger is a spiritual one. We hunger for a better quality rather than more quantity.

I would like to suggest a few ways to satisfy our spiritual hunger.

To provide nourishment for our starving mind and spirit, we must add new knowledge, wrestle with ideas, old and modern, learn new facts and develop new insight.

Amos speaks of the hunger for the words of God. We must study especially Torah. Torah flows through many different streams from the wellsprings of revelation and from the sources of our Jewish spiritual creativity. Torah holds treasures for everyone. Torah study is self-discovery. It is not the exploration of alien territory, but of your own spiritual history.

Torah will add Jewish depth to your life.

Another approach to greater contentment is Jewish observance. The fulfilment of Mitzvot imparts a sense of holiness to your life. Jewish deeds raise you above the level of the commonplace. You will not necessarily have more, but you will be more.

Observe the Shabbat. Shabbat is not just another day, but a day like no other. It is the day of contentment and of holiness, hallowing work and time.

Shabbat leads you to your Synagogue. It is the day to restore your connections to your family, to your community, and above all, to God.

If you want to escape from the compulsion of wanting more, train yourself to give, rather than to find ways to get! Giving, not receiving, is the antidote to excessive wanting.

41

Replace the futility of buying more things for yourself with buying into the lives of others. How do you pay for this investment? By giving of yourself.

"Love your fellow as yourself!" the Torah commands (Leviticus 19:18). As long as we only love ourselves, we shall never have enough. Loving others enriches us. Its rewards are deeper than those of self-indulgence.

How can you start loving others? Let me offer at least one suggestion.

Help your friends in need. Hopefully, they will not require material support, though that may also happen, but often people in your own circle may find themselves isolated by illness or sorrow. They may need you, just you. Neither gifts nor loans, nor anything money can buy.

Your friend may have suffered a bereavement. You and others were there during the "Shiv'a," the week of mourning. Now the Shiv'a is over and your friend very lonely. The visitors are gone. They left emptiness behind.

How often have men and women confided to me how lonely they felt after the loss of a spouse. "During the Shiv'a I had more company than I wanted," a widow tells me; "since then, nobody!"

The fellow human beings who depend on us more than anyone else are the members of our own family. Buying into their lives means to modify our own life in such a fashion that we will be there for them.

Be a father! Be a mother! Enter your children's or your grandchildren's lives in a real sense. You cannot do it by giving them more things.

Try to be a model for your children and grandchildren! Not a model to show them how to make money. Not a model to show them how to be a consumer on a big scale or how to be a smart shopper.

It is good and enjoyable to share recreational activities with your offspring. However, they need you not as their model on the tennis court or on the golf links!

Be a model to show them how to be a human being, a "mensch." Show them how to be a good Jew. Be their model in loving Jewish tradition; be their model in nobility, decency, respect of self and others. Be their model in loyalty to family, to our people and to our community. Be their model of responsibility.

A beautiful Midrash describes how God deliberated before he spoke to Moses for the very first time (Shmot Rabba 3:1).

How should his voice sound to Moses? If his voice were to be powerful and strong, Moses might be overwhelmed by the voice itself and fail to grasp what God wanted to communicate. If he were to speak in a gentle and soft voice, Moses might not hear God amidst all the distracting noises of the environment.

Said God: "I will speak to him *'b'kolo shel aviv'* - in his father's voice!"

Your voice can be God's voice to your children.

Be a model of Godliness to your family! That is the best you can give of your own self. It is the gift that may release you from the vicious cycle of incessant want. It may enable you to discover in your life the blessing for which we pray so fervently this day: "*Chayim Tovim*" - the life of goodness and of contentment.

On Truth, Justice and Peace

When the provincial government invited me to offer the Invocation at the Investiture Ceremony of the Order of Ontario, I accepted with pleasure. I was even more pleased when I looked at the list of the recipients on whom the Order was to be conferred.

The list covered a broad social spectrum.

The men and women to be honoured with the Order of Ontario ranged from individuals who had achieved distinction in the fields of art and science to a humble humanitarian whose career had begun as a railroad porter.

Perhaps I owe it to my occasional serendipity that the right Jewish source leaped into my mind. I like a text whose relevance is not too obvious at first glance. I based my invocation, a brief homily really, on an interpretation of the triad Truth, Justice and Peace.

On Truth, Justice and Peace
An Invocation at the Ceremony of Investiture of The Order of Ontario, May 9th 1988

The ancient sages of the Jewish tradition teach that society rests on three foundations: Truth, Justice and Peace.

Let us reflect on this theme as we begin the Investiture Ceremony of the Order of Ontario.

The men and women who are about to receive well deserved homage have gained distinction in the pursuit of these three ideals. If we agree that truth may be found not only in research and scholarly inquiry, but also in the artist's intuitive revelation of beauty; if we accept that the mandates of justice include the quest for human dignity and the release of minds enslaved by the imposition of ignorance; if we understand that peace is predicated on the amelioration of people's material condition and on humanity's liberation from hunger and preventable disease, then all of these honoured individuals have strengthened the everlasting foundations of our own society and enhanced the prospects for universal happiness. They have sharpened our focus on truth; they have refined our perception of justice; and they have applied to contemporary reality our vision of peace.

These men and women are our designers and builders, our dreamers and workers, our prophets and pioneers. Not only do they confer on us the benefits of their knowledge, skill, creativity, dedication and sacrifice, but they serve also as models of excellence, as paradigms of the human potential and as exemplars of genius.

They, Almighty God, represent man and woman created in your divine image. On them I invoke your blessing. Preserve in us, we pray, the ability to distinguish between mediocrity and excellence, to recognize genius and also to appreciate the true greatness of those who serve humbly and unselfishly. We ask you to bless the government and people of this Province and of this great and wonderful country, Canada. May Truth, Justice and Peace ever be her foundations. Amen.

The
SECOND
window

A Cry for Zion

My first sermon as Rabbi of Adath Israel

I preached my first sermon as Rabbi of my Congregation on the last Shabbat of the year 5707 (1946-7), having been engaged by the Congregation as of September the first, immediately before the Jewish New Year.

Adath Israel was then a small congregation, housed in a former church building next to King Edward School on Bathurst Street, just north of College Street. The membership numbered less than 200 families. I was expected to preach in Yiddish to accommodate the older worshippers. It took two years before the composition of the Shabbat congregation changed and I could switch to English.

In September of 1947, the agony of post-Holocaust European Jewry had risen to a fever pitch of desperation. Still considered "Displaced Persons" in the countries where they found themselves after liberation, the Holocaust survivors had one uppermost desire: to go to Palestine. Britain blocked the way. As the mandatory power, Britain had decided to savagely curtail Jewish immigration leaving the remnant of European Jewry without escape from the continent where their kin had perished and their communities had been wiped out. The British navy, controlling the Mediterranean, was determined to foil all attempts at "illegal" immigration, a policy that led to tragic confrontations and calamities.

Jewish leadership in the free world mobilized the maximum possible support for the demands of the "Yishuv," the Jewish settlement in Palestine, for increased immigration and for eventual statehood. In September, pressure had built up to an explosive degree. No one could predict that in less than three months, the United Nations General Assembly would adopt a partition plan predicated on the creation of a Jewish State in Palestine. In the meantime, the anguish of the Jewish people had plumbed new depths.

My first sermon, which is presented here in English translation, gave vent to the cataclysmic emotions of the time. The eyes of the Jewish people,

*and indeed the eyes of the world, were focussed on a ship named "Exodus."
The "Exodus" was preparing to sail from Italy to Palestine with a boatload
of survivors, in defiance of the British authorities and of the British navy
waiting to intercept the ship. It was one of the traumatic convulsions of
post-war Jewish history. Eventually, the voyage of the "Exodus" forced
the world community to end the Palestine stalemate.*

*As a 27-year-old man, who had himself escaped from Europe only eight
years before, my emotions of empathy and fury ran high. The intensity
of my feelings probably exceeded my immature preaching skills.*

A Cry for Zion
Preached on Parshat Nitzavim 5707
September 13, 1947,
Translated from the original Yiddish

> *You are standing today, all of you, before the Lord, your
> God* (Deuteronomy 29:9).

These words, the beginning of today's Torah reading, are the signal
that the final week of the fading year has arrived. Be prepared to
stand before God on the imminent High Holidays!

Today -a mere two days before Rosh Hashana- our minds should
focus entirely on the spiritual message of the High Holidays. Ex-
traneous subjects ought to be banished from our attention as
undesirable distractions. However, this is not an ordinary change
of year through which we are passing. It is exceptional. Today we
must shout from the roof tops the words of the Haftara which we
just finished reading:

> *For Zion's sake I will not be silent,*
> *And for Jerusalem I will not be still,*
> *Till her vindication will shine forth brilliantly,*
> *And her salvation as a flaming torch!* (Isaiah 62:1).

In this last phase of 5707, a time when according to Rabbinic tradition we have one last chance to make amends for the deficien-
cies of the past year, we witnessed a heart-rending tragedy for the
Jewish people.

I am referring to the fate of several thousand Jewish survivors from Europe who were desperate to settle in the Land of Israel. Not only did the British navy bar them from landing in Palestine, but they shipped them back to the hell of Europe from which they had fled, and forced them physically to step again on the earth which had soaked up the tears and the blood of their unfortunate brothers and sisters.

These sad events transpired during the last week of the old year when we cast about for favourable portends for the future. What irony that the Haftara for today is one of the "Seven Chapters of Consolation," in which the prophet Isaiah comforts us in our sorrow for Zion!

These poor survivors, who were forcibly dragged back to Germany, had chartered a boat to take them to the Land of Israel. Familiar with the story of the Exodus from Egypt three thousand years before, which had liberated their ancestors from Egyptian oppression, they wanted the name of their boat to reflect their own horror-filled history and, at the same time, to express their hope for the future. So they named their boat "Exodus," thus consigning their afflictions to a past they were leaving behind, and announcing their passage to a future of hope and rehabilitation.

Alas! In the historic Exodus from Egypt, when a recalcitrant Pharaoh attempted to force them back into captivity, his armies were drowned in the Sea of Reeds. It did not happen this time. This time, their enemies prevailed and cruelly returned them to the land of their bondage.

"For Zion's sake I will not be silent." How can we be still at this time?

One of our great mystics, the saintly Rabbi Isaac Luria, taught that because the souls of all Israelites are joined at their source, we have a great capacity for empathy. Yet we cannot fathom the despair of these unfortunate Jews. They are being denied the opportunity of a little peace in the land of Israel. They had hazarded everything for that last hope.

However, we feel very deeply how their sad experience epitomizes the plight of our entire Jewish people. In one word, our outlook is hopeless.

Can this be the omen for our future? Does the fate of the ship "Exodus from Europe" signify what we Jews face as we mark "Exodus 5707"? Does it foreshadow our new year?

What happened to the "Exodus" and her human cargo is a sharp reminder that our fate is still in the hands of others, as it has been throughout the last two thousand years. On the threshold of the year 5707, the political weakness of our Jewish people is driven home to us once again. *"The hands are the hands of Esaw"* (Genesis 27:22). As long as power decides the outcome, other nations will prevail over us.

And so, we stand before our God, *"with our forebears' craft in our hands,"* resorting to our traditional skill with prayer and repentance. We approach our problems with faith in the Psalmist's reassurance: *"Some trust in chariots, and some trust in horses, but we shall prevail in the name of the Lord, our God"* (Psalm 20:8). Other nations may rely on their military might; our strength comes from God.

A disturbing question puzzles me: how could the British, our traditional friends, act in this fashion? Has it never occurred to them that their own present troubles might be a sign from Heaven; that just as ancient Egypt was visited with plagues when the Egyptians stalled the Exodus of the Israelites, there might be a modern edition of the Ten Plagues in store for those who obstruct the Jewish Exodus from Europe?

I know that many Englishmen read the Bible frequently. Let us hope they will read the prophet Obadiah, who castigates the treachery of those who take no pity on survivors and turn fugitives away from their refuge. Or that they will read today's Haftara which describes the retribution exacted from those who oppress the Jewish people: *"Who is he that comes from Edom, with crimsoned garments from Bozrah?"* (Isaiah 63:1).

As for ourselves, let us read from the same Haftara the verses that herald the salvation of our people and our land. *"On your walls, o Jerusalem, I have positioned watchmen; all day, all night, they shall never fall silent"* (Isaiah 62:6). These sentries do not patrol the walls of Jerusalem to drive off the wretched fugitives seeking shelter, but to defend the Jewish people: *"Behold, the Lord has proclaimed to the end of the earth: Say to the daughter of Zion: 'behold, your salvation comes!'"* (62:11). Amen!

What a Difference a Psalm Makes!

In the classic Jewish sermon, it is the text that advances the thought. The litmus test which a good sermon must pass judges the preacher's success in selecting passages from the literature - Scripture, Talmud, Midrash and other classical works- that will supply the framework and the momentum for the development of the ideas he wishes to convey to his listeners.

Usually, the preacher draws on a class of texts called "Aggada," literally, "A Story Told." It is that half of our literary tradition that consists of lore, philosophy, nature, history, homiletical observations, legendary material. In other words, Aggada is everything that does not belong to the other half: "Halacha." Halacha -"the way to go"- is the prescriptive or legal tradition. It regulates conduct, thus dealing with the laws, the rules and the customs governing life and religious observance. For example, a Talmudic discussion regarding the nature of the booths in which the ancient Israelites dwelled during their desert journey, whether they were real huts or whether they refer to the protective shelter of supernatural clouds with which God surrounded them, is "Aggada." A discussion by the Talmudic Sages as to which materials are fit to cover the "Sukkah" -the ritual booth- is "Halacha."

My teacher, Rabbi Abraham A. Price, would sometimes observe that the true mark of quality in a sermon is the successful use of a legal text - Halacha- for the development of the theme. Unfortunately, this is a difficult and time-consuming assignment. The incentive to try is not compelling: few individuals in the average congregation are able to appreciate the originality, artistry and homiletical creativity involved in the process. On the rare occasions when I have used a Halachic passage in a sermon, my own satisfaction probably exceeded the congregation's.

"What a Difference a Psalm Makes!" is a good example of a Halacha-based sermon.

I was puzzled by a curious controversy between the ancient Academy of Hillel and that of Shammai. These two famous schools, founded by two dominant scholars of the early Rabbinic age, often took opposite stands on major issues in Jewish law, and occasionally on fundamental theological questions. [1]

In this instance, the controversy seemed to revolve around a minor point in the "Seder," literally the Order, the annual Passover ritual. The Seder includes a sacred meal as well as the formal narration of the Exodus from Egypt. Part of the prescribed liturgy is the recitation of the "Hallel," a string of thanksgiving psalms (Psalms 113-118). The tradition was, and still is, to divide the Hallel into two parts, the first to be recited before the meal, and the second afterwards. The two renowned academies of Hillel and Shammai disagree on the point whether one or two chapters of the Hallel should be recited before the meal.

What a trivial question for the two famous schools to debate! What earth-shaking difference does it make whether we recite the second psalm, Psalm 114, before or after the meal?

Once I concentrated on this question, it was not long before I discerned in the controversy between the schools the projection of a modern dilemma. It was as if the arguments of the disciples of Hillel and Shammai pre-figured a controversy that arose nearly 2000 years later, a controversy which has a great deal to do with the condition of our Jewish community today. The Hillel-versus-Shammai dispute highlights a tendency in the psyche of Jewish North America.

Does that mean I believe that the ancient rabbinic scholars were actually anticipating our time and had a prescient knowledge of modern conditions? Of course not. I am not at all sure that the insight I derived from this Talmudic text was in fact in the minds of the Sages who debated the place of Psalm 114 in the order of the Passover celebration. Nevertheless, my analysis is a legitimate homiletical hypothesis and illustrates a sermonic technique which achieves two valid purposes: firstly, to explore seriously and searchingly a curious legal rabbinic text; and secondly, to use it in an attempt to modify a contemporary attitude which is detrimental to our behaviour as Jews.

It is an attitude that puzzled and disturbed me almost from the moment I arrived in Toronto in 1942.

Having been raised in Germany, I remembered the appalling degree of assimilation that had prevailed in the Jewish community in Germany. The low level of Jewishness I found in my new home did not come as a shock to me, therefore. It did not surprise me to see Jews ignoring and neglecting Jewish observance and learning. I had seen enough of that in Germany. What did perplex me was the acquiescence on the part of observant Jewish immigrants toward the abandonment of Judaism by their own children. Jews who in their own conduct and thinking were true to the tradition they had absorbed in Eastern Europe tolerated and even encouraged the rise of a generation that was Jewishly ignorant and non-observant.

The result was a dismal, depressed condition of Jewish religious and spiritual life. To remedy this condition was the main challenge of the rabbinate at the time of my ordination. Fortunately, there followed a marked improvement in Jewish education and a return to higher levels of participation in Jewish life, particularly in the Synagogue community. Nevertheless, the consequences of the earlier attitudes are still very much with us.

Many of my sermons dealt with the phenomenon of the "Lost Generation." However, in the sermon "What a Difference a Psalm Makes!" I was able to discuss the problem with a degree of originality that I owed to a fortuitous interpretation of the Hillel-Shammai debate.

What a Difference a Psalm Makes! ───────
Preached on Passover 5741 - 1981

עד היכן הוא אומר? בית שמאי אומרים עד אם הבנים
שמחה. ובית הלל אומרים עד חלמיש למעינו מים.

How far should one recite (the Hallel before the meal)? The School of Shammai taught: Up to "A Mother joyful with children" (Psalm 113:9). The School of Hillel taught: Up to "The flint stone into a fountain of water" (Psalm 114:8).
(Mishna Pesachim 10:6)

The text of my sermon, from the Mishna of the Tractate "Pesachim," addresses the question how much of the "Hallel," a collection of Psalms of Praise, is to be recited at the Seder before we eat the Matza, the Maror and serve the meal. By this point in the ritual, the story of the Exodus has been told; the meaning of Matza, of the bitter vegetables and of the Passover lamb have been explained. The participants in the Seder have been stimulated to re-live the Exodus experience. Now, in the order of the ritual, we are to recite the Hallel, to give praise and thanks for redemption. The Hallel is recited on all the festivals of the year, but it is most closely associated with Passover and is an integral part of the Seder.

But there is a problem. The children around the Seder Table, whose participation is so essential, are hungry and tired by this time. If we do not hurry they may be asleep before they have had a chance to eat the Matza and taste the Maror. So we must shorten the recitation of the Hallel, reciting only a part before the meal, and leaving the rest for after the meal.

The question is, how much must we recite before the meal? How far can we go before the children will become too impatient or drop off to sleep?

The Shammaites hold that we recite only one Psalm before the meal, the first one, ending with the words "*A mother joyful with children.*" A beautiful Psalm it is, indeed! It sings that God "*raises the poor from the dust; from the dunghill he elevates the needy, to seat him with the princes, with the princes of his people...*" That's how far we go, says the School of Shammai. That's enough! If you recite more, the kids will either protest or tune out and soon be asleep!

The School of Hillel disagrees. The children may be tired, hungry, and perhaps even bored; all the same, you must include also the second Psalm while they are still awake waiting for the meal. This Psalm celebrates the drama of the Exodus: "*When Israel came forth from Egypt, the House of Jacob from an alien folk, Judah became his holy nation, Israel his domain. When the sea saw it, it fled; the Jordan turned backward.*" This Psalm, enthralled by Israel's miraculous history, extols its election as God's very own people, and glories in the wonders during its trek through the wilderness where God "*turned the rock into a pool of water; the flint stone into a fountain of water.*"

We follow the teaching of Hillel. We recite both Psalms before the meal.

What is the significance?

Passover is the festival of History. It summons us to identify with

56

our past. Yet at the same time, Passover anticipates our future. We are to perceive a design in history.

Life is not a repetitive sequence of replays. There is movement, progress, the unfolding of the new. We must take our place in the forward-marching column of our people.

Passover, therefore, highlights generational linkage. The Torah commands us -and the Seder ritual implements this obligation- to explain the past to our children. When your children ask you, tell them the story. If they don't, take the initiative yourself and tell them.

As the debate between the schools of Shammai and Hillel indicates, the Seder is the one ritual shaped essentially by the needs of the youngest participants. The reason for its many curious practices is *"to make the children ask questions."* We want to bring our children into the stream of history and imbue them with a sense of continuous peoplehood.

A grandfather recently told me with beaming enthusiasm of the beautiful Seder his family enjoyed. "My fifteen-year old granddaughter conducted it all," he proudly proclaimed. I sincerely congratulated him. I knew that he himself, though an elder in age, would not have been able to lead the ritual or recite the Hebrew text of the Haggada! What good fortune to have such a learned granddaughter!

Interesting, how in some families children have exchanged roles with their parents or grandparents! The intended recipients of the tradition have become its transmitters to their elders. These families are fortunate, of course. Regrettably, there is a greater number of families where the art and skill of conducting a traditional Seder has been irretrievably lost to indifference and ignorance.

How did that happen? What was the reason for the breakdown of generational linkage? Why did so many members of the Jewish immigrant community fail to pass on our tradition and the means for keeping it alive and vibrant? Why did the passing of the immigrant patriarch leave such a void in so many Jewish families? Why was the history of the North American Jewish community characterized for so many decades by a deepening ignorance of Torah and an increasing neglect of observance? And why may it be premature to ask that question in the past tense, as if the trend had already been successfully reversed?

The reason was that the immigrant patriarch and matriarch - the venerated Zaide, himself a model of piety and scholarship, and the adorable Bubbe, a paradigm of self-denial and love - followed the School of Shammai rather than that of Hillel.

Why bother the children with the tales of long ago? Who needs history, the Exodus, the "Bubbe-maisses" of miracles - the burden of the second Psalm of Hallel? It will make the kids fall asleep! The first chapter is enough: *"God raises the poor from the dust, the needy from the dung-hill, seating him with the princes..."* That is the Torah of America; that is our faith! We were poor, at the low end of the social ladder, and now we are making it. We are upwardly mobile. We will soon have reached the rung of the elite; we shall soon sit with the princes of society!

It took a few generations before we realized that without the second chapter, the first chapter of the Hallel is incomplete. It is not enough to have been raised from the dung-hill to heights of affluence. We are empty inside without the experience of *"When Israel went forth from Egypt ..."* We have failed if we do not repeat *"Judah became his holy people."*

There are signals of a Jewish spiritual revival. Young people are returning to authenticity. While disparaging critics of North American Jewry used to describe the Jewish scene as an arid wasteland, the *"rocks"* are turning *"into fountains of water,"* generating new streams of Torah which change a desert into seed beds of creativity.

What better time to join this revolution than the festival of liberation! As our ancestors went from darkness to light, let us follow the lead of many of our children and proceed from indifference to commitment, from alienation to redemption. Let us restore the linkage between the generations. Let us raise a generation that will not fall asleep at the contemplation of history! Let us have faith in the relevance of holiness. Let us follow the School of Hillel and embrace the difference a Psalm makes!

[1] *See "Is Life Worthwhile?" - page 4*

A Tale of Two Walls

In March of 1984, I visited Germany at the invitation of the Government of the Federal Republic. My visit was the sequel of a previous visit to the land of my birth. Two years earlier, I had returned to my home town, Cologne-Mülheim, as the guest of Christian churches. My official itinerary had not extended beyond Cologne. Now the West German government wanted me to have a first-hand look at the new Jewish communities and to see a greater part of the new democratic Germany.

One of the highlights of my tour was my first-ever visit to Berlin. My deep impressions of that experience formed the substance of a sermon shortly after my return to Toronto.

Subsequent events have rather enhanced the relevance of that sermon. The reunification of Germany, the dissolution of the Communist empire and its as yet unforeseeable consequences have given the sermon a renewed significance.

In retrospect, the sermon seems to have been brushed with a prophetic patina. It ended on a hopeful note.

A Tale of Two Walls
A Sermon preached on Parshat Hachodesh [1] 5744 - 1984

*T*he month of liberation is here, the month of Messianic hope!

To explain the significance of the season beginning today, our ancient Sages quote a verse from the *"Song of Songs"* and use the verse to spin a curious conversation between the people Israel and the future Messiah.

> *"Hark! the voice of my lover! He is about to come!..*
> *He stands behind our wall" (Song of Songs 2:8,9) - this*
> *verse refers to the Messianic King. When he comes and*
> *announces to the people Israel "In this month you will*
> *be redeemed," they will say to him: "O our Master,*
> *Messianic King! How can we be redeemed? Did our Holy*
> *God not say that he will subject us to bondage at the*
> *hands of all the seventy nations of the world?" (Pesikta*
> *Rabbati 15:71)*

"Our exile is not finished yet," the Jews will say. "Some empires haven't had their turn yet to oppress us. We have not completed God's sentence. We have only had the Babylonians, the Persians, the Greeks and the Romans! We have to wait until all the other nations have had their turn!"

> *The Messiah will then give them two replies:*

> *"You need not suffer the misery of exile under each*
> *of the world's nations! If only one of you will be exiled*
> *to Barbaria* 2 *and another one to Sarmatia, it will be*
> *reckoned as if you all had gone there into exile.*

> *Furthermore, the Roman empire conscripts legions from*
> *all the foreign nations. A contingent of Kuteans will come*
> *and oppress you, and it will be considered as if their whole*
> *nation had oppressed you. Therefore, in this month will*
> *you be redeemed!" (Pesikta Rabbati 15:71)*

What an interesting idea! We may serve exile by proxy. We may delegate a part of society to pay the fine for all the rest. The affliction of each one of us is counted in the total of the punishment we have been collectively condemned to bear.

I had a very strange experience while visiting Berlin a few weeks ago. Walking through the divided city, I could not stop humming and singing in my head Naomi Shemer's beautiful song of "*Yerushalayim shel Zahav* - Jerusalem of Gold." Annoyed, I tried to get the words and the tune out of mind, but I could not. They seemed so inappropriate, even blasphemous, in my surroundings. But I could not stop humming the line *"ha-ir asher badad yoshevet uv'libah choma - the city that dwells in loneliness, and in her heart - a wall."*

These beautiful words belong only to Jerusalem, the city of the spirit, the city of light, the place where heaven and earth touch and embrace!

The Wall, of which the song speaks, was revered for centuries as the only visible remains of the Holy Temple. This wall is the heart of Jerusalem. Here converge the prayers of all Israel. Here emanates the spirit of holiness to warm the world with blessing and peace. From this vestige of the Temple, so the tradition goes, God's glory had never departed. A shred of God's own presence clung to the stones of this wall through all the storms of fire and pillage, through all the conquests and devastations.

But I was not in Jerusalem. I was in Berlin, the city that not so many years ago had been the metropolis of darkness, the capital of the grossest evil. From here, the legions of death and destruction had been unleashed upon the world.

Somehow, the city of Berlin, isolated from the rest of Germany and divided by its infamous wall, had triggered in my subconsciousness the song of Jerusalem and its sacred wall.

As the Western Wall in Jerusalem is symbolic of holiness and spirituality, so conversely the Berlin wall overwhelmed me as the epitome of evil, an obscene distillation of filth.

First, I saw the wall from street level. A tall concrete barrier; the end of the world. "Stop!" it says. "This is the ultimate dead end." The wall is arrogant, insulting. What is on the other side? you wonder.

My second view of the wall was from an elevated vantage point. Right near the wall, the famous German publisher Axel Springer had built his high-rise corporate headquarters. I had been invited to visit the impressive building, home of many West German newspapers. There is a press lounge on the top floor of the building and from that high elevation, I looked once more at the wall.

What a shock!

Behind the concrete barrier, which is all you see from street level, there is a vast expanse of no-man's land, a death strip with watch towers, patrol roads and a wide belt of black earth, like an ugly scar running through the heart of this huge city, as far as the eye can see, from horizon to horizon.

It is a frightening, terrifying vista. "Crime and punishment," my host said to me. "This is the area where Hitler built his monumental government buildings, the ministries and the chancellery. Here, all the diabolical crimes against humanity were planned. This was the centre of the Third Reich! And here is our punishment:

a giant slash through the heart of Berlin, and continuing along the whole border between east and west."

Later on, I took a bus tour of East Berlin. It was very interesting, but what I shall remember most was the sight of border guards checking the bus before it was allowed to return to the West. They even searched the underside of the bus with mirrors attached to poles which they poked underneath the vehicle, just in case someone might try to hide there to smuggle himself out of the Communist paradise. Thousands of years ago, the Chinese built a mighty wall to keep invaders out; East Germany built a wall to keep its people in!

I had no reason to feel sorry for the post-war division of Germany. But I felt that this horrible wall does more than divide Germany and Berlin.

This wall, I felt, goes right through the heart of humanity.

This wall symbolizes everything that divides human beings. That ugly black scar, that cruel slash, epitomizes all the hatred and all the hostility that tear mankind apart.

We are all victims of the wall. Religious fanaticism, inbred chauvinism, teachings of supremacy and traditional grudges handed down from one generation to the next continue to bring untold suffering to people on this earth. How senseless! How foolish!

The divided city stands for all the self-inflicted evils of the world. It is proxy for the exile of humanity. As the Messiah says about the lonely Jew suffering exile in Barbaria: "He represents all of you; he is paying your fine." The wall through Berlin sums up all the hatred, the alienation, the tyranny, the cruelty and the divisiveness of human society.

Therefore, it must be time for the Messiah! It must be time for healing, for uniting and for bringing us all together!

We need not say, "Our exile is not finished yet. The debt has not yet been paid. There are still varieties of misery and catastrophe we have not sampled yet."

No; we have been through it all. If we did not suffer in our own person the full spectrum of the deadly hatreds, enough of us did. We had proxies. Not only Jews. Somewhere, some of us suffered every variation of the consequences of human perversity: slaughter, torture, starvation, isolation and nuclear incineration.

Enough already! A new month, the first in the calendar of liberation, is upon us!

Let there be a new beginning!

1 *Parshat Hachodesh is a special Torah portion (Exodus 12) read on the last Sabbath before the New Moon of Nissan, the Passover month, or on the New Moon itself, if it falls on the Sabbath. It begins with the words: "This month shall be for you the first of the months .."*

2 *"Barbaria" may refer to any non-Roman, therefore "barbarian" country. In another version of this Midrash, Britania is mentioned in place of Sarmatia (Yalkut Shimoni).*

Jethro:
a Eulogy for
Rabbi Albert
Pappenheim

"Hesped" is the Hebrew word for a funeral sermon. The word means "lament," a verbal outpouring of grief, but it also has a causative connotation: a catharsis for mourners to vent their grief. It is therefore not identical with "eulogy."

Traditionally, the Hesped utilizes the exposition of a Torah text to develop its thought, and in this respect it resembles a sermon. A Hesped is also intended to honour the departed. This objective is achieved most effectively, in the Jewish way of thinking, if his or her achievements can be described or illustrated in terms of a text from the traditional literature.

Rabbi Albert Pappenheim, of Beth David Bnai Israel Beth Am Congregation, Toronto, was an old friend. A few weeks before his death after a long and painful illness he asked me while I was visiting him to hold the eulogy at his funeral. It was a painful moment for both of us. For me it was also a great honour, a tribute to a friendship of more than forty years and the expression of a deep and important trust.

I met Albert Pappenheim in 1938. We were fellow students at the Jewish Teachers Seminary in Würzburg till its destruction during Crystal Night in November of the same year. For a week, we shared a jail cell in Würzburg; then I was sent to Dachau, while he being two years younger was sent home. We met again at the Yeshivah Torath Emeth in London; we were interned together and eventually resumed our parallel lines of study at the Yeshivah Torath Chaim in Toronto and at the University of Toronto. Later on, we were rabbinical colleagues at two Toronto Synagogues in the same suburban neighbourhood.

We knew each other's thoughts and inclinations and could in light moments tease one another about our emotional differences and intellectual idiosyncrasies. Above all, we could talk to each other with the utmost candour. We were very much like brothers.

I approached the task of composing a "Hesped" for my friend with awe and with love. To be frank, I also felt as if a higher creative spirituality was guiding my thoughts and enabled me to develop a portrait of my lost friend on the basis of the Torah portion of the week. Perhaps Albert himself helped me write the eulogy. I am sure in his humility he would have disagreed with the content, but he would have appreciated the "Torah."

Jethro:
A Memorial Tribute to Rabbi Albert Pappenheim at his funeral on January 19, 1984

Albert!

צר לי עליך אחי יהונתן נעמת לי מאד

The words in my aching heart are the words of David lamenting his friend *"I grieve for you, my brother Jonathan; you were very dear to me"* (II Samuel 1:26). *"I grieve - 'tzar li'* [1] *- for myself"*, for the painful personal loss which so many others share with me; for you were dear to me as my *brother*; and *'alecha'* - *I grieve for you, for your sake,"* for your tragedy. You had to leave behind prematurely so much of what you were able to accomplish and create. I also grieve for all you had to leave undone, for the hopes you were not given to fulfil in the 62 years of your life and for the plans whose realization death denied you.

The Torah portion of this week is named after "Jethro" - Yitro in Hebrew - the father-in-law of Moses. In the "Mechilta," an ancient Rabbinic commentary on the text (Exodus 18:1), we read:

שבעה שמות נקראו לו: יתר, יתרו ,חובב, רעואל, חבר,
פוטיאל, קני. יתר, שהותיר פרשה אחת בתורה. יתרו
שייתר במעשים טובים. חובב, שהיה חביב למקום.
רעואל, שהיה כריע למקום . חבר, שנעשה כחבר למקום.
פוטיאל, שנפטר מעבודה זרה. קני, שקנא לשמים וקנה לו
תורה.

He was called by seven names: Yeter, Yitro, Hovav, Re'uel, Hever, Putiel and Keini.

65

"He was called Yeter," a name which comes from a word meaning 'to be more, to add,' *"because he added one extra chapter to the Torah,"* namely the first chapter of this week's Torah portion. This chapter relates how Jethro suggested important administrative improvements to Moses. In return God honoured Jethro by adding to the Torah this chapter bearing Jethro's name.

"He was called Yitro," from the same root 'to be more,' *"because he abounded in good deeds."* A parallel passage in the same Midrash explains, *"Originally, people called him only 'Yeter,' but after he had done good deeds, a letter was added to his name, similar to Abraham, who was originally called Abram; when he became known for good deeds, a letter was added so that his name became Abraham,"* the Hebrew name of our friend Rabbi Albert Pappenheim.

"He was called Hovav," a word meaning 'beloved' *"because he was beloved by God; he was called Re'uel,"* a merger of the word for friend and the word God, *"because he was as a friend to God; his name was Hever,"* from a root meaning 'to be associated with, to accompany,' *"because he became as a companion, a 'Chaver,' to God; he was also named Putiel,"* a name the sages relate to the verb 'patar - to take leave, to depart', *"because he departed from idolatry, from 'Avoda Zara;'* his name was also Keini"* which the Sages associate with 'kana - zeal' and 'kanah - to buy, to acquire' *"because he was zealous for the sake of heaven and because he acquired Torah."*

May I be permitted to pay tribute to Rabbi Albert Pappenheim under the rubrics of these names.

Let the first name be "Keini," a "Kenite". It is a gentilic name, identifying a member of the Kenite tribe, to which Moses' father-in-law belonged. It was a tribe of nomads, of wanderers. Their tribal name traces their ancestry to Cain, the eternal fugitive, roaming homeless across the earth.

Young Albert Pappenheim, for the first 35 years of his life, was a "Keini," a homeless wanderer. Born in Frankfurt-on-Main, a renowned German-Jewish community, he was raised close to the heartbeat of Jewish life. His father served in a professional capacity in one of the most distinguished Synagogues of the city. In Frankfurt, while he received his early education, the shadow of the Nazi regime fell over his life; subsequently, he attended the Jewish Teachers Seminary in Würzburg.

During "Crystal Night" November 10, 1938, the Seminary was

destroyed. Albert eventually made his way to London, England, where he enrolled at the Yeshivah Torath Emeth. Yet his wanderings were far from over. Together with thousands of other refugees, he was interned in Britain as a German national and shipped to Canada, where he spent nearly two years in internment camps. Finally, he was released through the efforts of Rabbi Abraham A. Price and reached Toronto where he became a student at the Yeshivah Torah Chaim.

However, these were not only years of wandering. They were also the years *"sheh-kinnei lashamayim v'kana lo tora,"* the years marked *"by zeal for Heaven and by the acquisition of Torah."* They were years of growing attachment to the Jewish heritage. It was during this period of his life that he acquired his share of Torah and decided to dedicate his life to Judaism. In addition to his studies at the Yeshivah he studied at the University of Toronto. It was because of this acquisition of Torah and of his serious commitment to Judaism and the Jewish people that he was ordained by Rabbi Price of Toronto; it was because of his zeal for Torah and Jewish education that he became the principal of the Dovercourt Synagogue Talmud Torah. He was rabbi in St. Catherines for four years; for two more years he served the congregation of Lexington, Kentucky. Finally, in 1956, his years as "Keini," as wanderer, came to an end. He returned to Toronto to become the rabbi of this Synagogue, Beth David, then a small, struggling suburban congregation.

And so, Keini became "Hovav," a name that means "beloved" and "loving," combining an active and a passive formation. He became not only *"beloved to God"* but literally, *"Lamakom - to the place,"* [2] his congregation. Rabbi Pappenheim had a strong capacity for love, to give it and to extend love to others, and he was universally beloved by others, widely admired and held in the highest esteem.

There was a deep relationship of love between Albert and his family. In Albert's lexicon, *"Hibba - love"* was related -as indeed it may be etymologically- to *"Hova - duty, responsibility."* Love and responsibility grew from the same root. Love must turn into duty. Bonds forged initially by love mature to form bonds of ongoing responsibility; love ripens in sacrifice, in caring, sharing, serving and giving. He was devoted without reservation to his wife, Rhoda. He had deep love for his siblings, his brother Ernst and sister Karla in Israel, and for his sister Ruth and brother-in-law Leo Posen. Because love becomes "Hova," reponsibility, he helped them after the war to re-establish themselves in Canada, in St. Catherines.

He had a most beautiful, indeed unique, relationship of love with his mother, Bubbie Sonia Kabatznik. I cannot call her a mother-in-law; she was his mother. It was a relationship that could have been created only by special people under special circumstances. I have never seen the like of it. They understood each other so well; they loved each other so whole-heartedly; they shared together the trials and the 'Nachas,' the sorrows and the joys. It was Hibbah, love, of the most beautiful and sacred kind.

Similar love was extended to his sisters-in-law, Diane and Cecile, and to his nieces and nephews.

The culmination of Hibbah and Hova, of love and responsibility, was his relationship with his precious daughter, Irma. How he cared for her; how he loved her; how he found time to spend with her; how they shared precious moments and hours! They grew close together; they became so deeply attached to each other. He was a supportive father for Irma; he did not restrain her individuality and yet he taught her, by example, through the osmosis of his intuitive ability to communicate with her. Finally, when fate reversed the roles, Irma showed how well she had understood and accepted her father's teaching of "Hova" and "Hibba," love and duty. It was her turn to assume responsibility for her beloved Daddy's care during the long period of illness. She was at his bedside always, until the very moment he drew his last breath.

Indeed he was Hovav, the person of love and responsibility.

Rabbi Pappenheim also merits another name of Jethro's, the name "Yeter: he who adds, *"she-hotir parasha achat - because he added"* and *"preserved,"* another meaning of *"hotir," "a chapter of the Torah."* Rabbi Pappenheim added more than one; he wrote many chapters of Torah on the hearts and minds of the people who were touched by his ministry as Rabbi, a teacher of Torah. He was a great scholar in his own right. The width and depth of his scholarship were often hidden beneath his unassuming demeanour. His scholarship was distinguished by its special soundness. There were no pyrotechnics; he did not care for superficial brilliance to compensate for a lack of substance. He did not indulge much in imaginative flights of loose speculation or in esoteric philosophy, but preferred the pursuit of solid, substantial knowledge.

He used a similarly sound approach in teaching. Along with love of Torah he communicated an appreciation of substance and of facts that you could take home with you and remember.

Jewish education was his special concern, both in his own Synagogue and as Chairman of the Education Commission of the United Synagogue, Ontario Region, a position in which he served effectively for several years.

His Torah ranged far and wide. He was an eclectic reader and an expert in many areas of human enquiry, Jewish and secular. His erudition was almost encyclopedic. "Hazanut" was a special love of his. In Cantorial music, as in music in general, he had accumulated considerable expertise. His learning was always well organized, methodical and systematic.

There was one special chapter in the Torah which he was most anxious to preserve, a chapter whose survival he felt was his special mission. This was the chapter written, and the history made, by the German-Jewish community. It was very important to him personally to preserve the customs, the *"Minhagim,"* the peculiar nuances of German Jewry. He was proud to be a "Yecke." He wanted to make sure that this German-Jewish portion of the Torah would be preserved through him and through others who shared his appreciation.

Rabbi Pappenheim became *"Re'uel, the friend of God,"* or, if we may connect the word with a similar Hebrew root, the *"shepherd of God."* God tests Jewish leaders, the Sages taught, by putting them in charge of a flock of sheep. Before he became the liberator and lawgiver, Moses was a shepherd; David was a shepherd long before he became king.

Albert had all the attributes of a shepherd. He was kind and gentle; he was caring and responsible, not just for people in the collective sense, but caring and responsible for the individual. As first Rabbi of this congregation, he was its faithful shepherd for 28 years. A devoted, sincere counsellor, a planner and problem-solver, he was the kindest shepherd that God could have appointed over his flock, attentive always to people's personal needs, commending and praising, encouraging and thus inspiring.

His function as shepherd went beyond the boundaries of the congregation. He faithfully served the United Synagogue, Ontario Region, as an active member and as a professional director for several years. It was always his aim to raise the standards of Jewish observance. Thus, he was largely responsible for the introduction of Bar Mitzvah standards and several other improvements in the organized religious life of the community.

The same soundness he brought to scholarship, he brought to congregational and communal leadership. He had no use for empty verbiage. Words had to have real meaning and had to lead to action.

Rabbi Pappenheim was active in Interfaith Dialogue. He made it his personal mission, in a quiet, effective way, to interpret Judaism to Christians without apology, without varnish, but truthfully and down-to-earth, in practical and in real human terms.

His name was also *"Hever, sheh-naasa k'chever lamakom"* - a companion to God, and to men, a true Chaver to myself and to many others. He was one of the oldest Chaverim I had. He was seventeen when I met him for the first time. We travelled the same road together; after short periods of separation, our tracks would soon converge again. He was with me in Würzburg; he was my study-partner, my "Chavruse," at the Yeshivah in London. While we daily studied Talmud together, he was not only my Chaver, but in many ways my teacher. I learned a great deal from him.

His "Chavership," his collegiality, extended to all members of the Rabbinate in our region. He was an active Chaver in the Toronto Board of Rabbis, and served several terms as chairman of the Ontario Region of the Rabbinical Assembly, a position he held at the time of his death. He was a Chaver not only to his colleagues but to congregants as well. Everybody considered him a friend. His talent for friendship was complemented by his wonderful sense of humour, his dry intelligent wit and his gift of seeing the lighter side of things. Even in serious situations his sense of humourous perspective never failed. He could toss off rhymes and poetry at will. His love for music and singing relaxed any stiff formality in personal relations.

And what a Chaver he was to his professional colleagues in his congregation! Not only to his Assistant Rabbi Philip Scheim and to the Chazanim, but also to the persons in the office who worked with him for so many years. They were friends, Chaverim; they were companions and fellows with deep mutual trust and loyalty. And they protected and sustained him in the months of illness.

And then he was *"Putiel: sheh-niftar mei-avoda zara - who removed himself from idolatry,"* from false worship, or, as a parallel Midrash puts it, *"sheh-pitpet ba-avoda zara - who despised the worship of false gods."* His intellectual integrity was uncompromising, as was his moral rectitude. He never was led astray by the false gods of popular modernity; he despised superficial fads. The trendy intellectual fashions of the day never tempted him to join the crowd running after the idol of the year. Not for him were the cheap slogans and buzz words of cut-rate communication. He removed himself from "Avoda Zara," the worship of false gods.

I remember a conversation in the sixties in which he disparaged the then popular notion of "relevance." Everything had to be "relevant" according to the gospel of the day: religion, ritual and worship! How he despised these superficial slogans, convinced that true relevance comes from within, rather than from temporary popularity. When it became popular for Rabbis to shed the rabbinic gown, in an outburst of superficial egalitarianism, he chose to retain it. On the other hand, he did not idolize slavish traditionalism. He was as critical of blind conformity to precedent as he was of idolizing innovation. Neither the past nor the present could dictate to him and supplant his own judgement.

The greatest "Avoda Zara" which he eschewed, the false god from which he distanced himself, deliberately and conscientiously, was the worst idolatry we know: worship of self. The sin of conceit and of pride was an "Avoda Zara" that he held in utter contempt.

He deflated not only the idols of the public, but he also deliberately diminished his own self. Humility was the hallmark of his personality. So humble, simple and modest was he that much of the recognition he deserved was not given to him; he became a true unselfish servant of God and of human beings.

Because of his humility he also avoided another vice which our Jewish tradition holds to be the equivalent of idol worship: anger. I cannot remember Rabbi Pappenheim ever displaying anger. Neither did he talk evil of anyone, for in his humility he could not think evil of anyone. The instructions he gave me and others regarding his funeral also reflected his modesty. He wanted a simple funeral, without theatrics, the same as any Jew in this congregation would be given.

Finally, his name - the name of this Torah portion - was *Yitro: "when he excelled in good deeds, people added the letter 'vav' to his name,"* changing it from Yeter to Yitro. Rabbi Pappenheim's good deeds added to his name: his fame grew, he received added recognition and tribute in the course of his life. Letters were added to his name: his first academic achievement, the B.A. in Oriental Languages from the University of Toronto. They were followed by the M.A., from the same University, to mark his advanced scholarship. Finally, came the letters D.D., indicating the Doctorate of Divinity from the Jewish Theological Seminary honouring him for his *"ma' asim tovim* - good deeds," as a leader of the Jewish community whose deeds were blessings for the Jewish people and for Israel.

And now we are about to add more letters to his name. We add *"Zayin Tzade Lamed: zecher tzadik liv-racha - may the memory of this righteous man be a blessing."* May his memory abide as a blessing to his family; a blessing to all who walked in the sunlight of his love and who passed through the sphere of his interest and concern.

May the memory of this righteous person be a blessing for each of us, inspiring, challenging and heartening, calling us to grow through sacrifice, to grow through service; to grow in our capacity to give, to be patient, to be forbearing, and to accept suffering as he did. May these letters added to his name inspire his congregation, its members and its leadership. May his memory especially inspire Rabbi Philip Scheim, who has been remarkably strong throughout these months of trouble and trial and whose rise to greatness was due in no small measure to the encouragement that he received from Rabbi Albert Pappenheim. May all of us be blessed by Rabbi Pappenheim's memory!

Albert, my friend, my teacher, my mentor in Torah and good deeds, my Chaver, let your memory be a blessing for me, *"na'amta li m'od -for you were so dear to me,"* and I shall miss you; and *"may your soul be bound up with ours in the bond of life eternal,"* as your memory guides us toward righteousness and love. Amen.

---

[1] *The Hebrew text counterpoints the 1st and the 2nd person, literally "there is distress to me for you."*

[2] *In Rabbinic literature, the word "Makom - Place" is often substituted, as here, for "God," God being "the place of the world."*

Bezalel: a Eulogy for Rabbi Stuart E. Rosenberg

⚫️ ⚫️ ◯ ◯

During the 1960s, a dominant personality on the Toronto Jewish scene was Dr. Stuart Rosenberg, Senior Rabbi of Beth Tzedec Synagogue. Under his leadership, Beth Tzedec, created by the merger of two well-established major Toronto congregations, grew into a powerful centre of Jewish cultural, spiritual, educational and social life, while the Rabbi himself was recognized as a prolific author and consummate speaker and teacher. Both Rabbi Rosenberg and his Synagogue made a strong beneficial impact on the entire community in many areas.

Rabbi Rosenberg was also a controversial individual. Unfortunately, his relationship to his congregation was terminated after a well-publicized legal battle. The negative repercussions of his bitter struggle with the congregational authorities have reverberated for many years in the Toronto Jewish community.

Eventually, Dr. Rosenberg assumed the spiritual leadership of Beth Torah Congregation while he continued with other aspects of his career. Regrettably, his health declined and limited his scope. He died at the age of 62 years.

Bezalel: a Eulogy for Rabbi Dr. Stuart E. Rosenberg ———————— *at his funeral on March 15, 1990*

Feelings of sadness and awe mingle in my heart as we hold this memorial for *Moreinu V'rabbeinu* -our Master, our Teacher- Rabbi Dr. Stuart E. Rosenberg; as I approach the pulpit elevated by his

Torah, as I stand on the Bema hallowed by his service, in the Synagogue that was the scene of his ministry.

Is it coincidence that this week's Torah portion portrays in terms so descriptive of Stuart the person who is our Biblical paradigm of creativity, artistry, intuition, skill and wisdom: Bezalel, the builder of the Tabernacle?

> *I have endowed him with a divine spirit of wisdom, understanding, knowledge and every skill; with the power to think thoughts ....* (Exodus 31:3)

These were some of the attributes, talents and abilities wondrously concentrated in one uniquely endowed individual, a great man, a giant personality, a creative and charismatic leader. He had the power to think thoughts, not mundane, ordinary, puny thoughts, but great ideas, daring concepts, brilliant visions!

> *Said Rav Judah in the name of Rav: "Bezalel knew how to combine the letters by which Heaven and Earth were created."* (B'rachot 55a)

That was Stuart's art. Rabbi Rosenberg had a miraculous gift of literary creativity; he was the spell-binding orator, the prolific writer who knew how to create worlds of thought and imagination by the combination of letters.

The meaning of the name *"Bezalel"* derives from *"B'zel-el: in the shadow of God."*

> *Rabbi Shmuel bar Nahmeini said in the name of Rabbi Yohanan,"Bezalel received his name because of his wisdom." When God instructed Moses to tell Bezalel to build "a tabernacle, a shrine and sacred vessels," Moses reversed the order when he relayed the message to Bezalel and told him to build "a shrine, vessels and a tabernacle." Said Bezalel to him: "Moses, our Teacher, the custom of the world is that a person first build the house and then bring in the furnishings, but you tell me to make first a shrine, vessels, and then a tabernacle! Where am I to put the vessels you ask me to make? Did God perhaps tell you thus, 'Tabernacle, shrine, vessels?'" Said Moses: "Were you perhaps right there in God's shadow so that indeed you know what God truly wanted?"* (ibid)

Stuart Rosenberg, the thinker, the dreamer, the craftsman, knew as Moses did that the content is more important than the container. He did not deny the superiority of the idea, the essence and the spirit, over the form. But part of his genius was his creative conviction that great ideas require great institutions.

He was certain that Jewish values require a great Synagogue to nurture and sustain them; that scholarship requires outstanding schools; that great thoughts call for appropriate opportunities to present them.

That was why he involved himself, with imagination and vision, and with spectacular success, in the creation of a great Synagogue institution as the abode of great Jewish values; in the creation of a Synagogue Museum as the home of an outstanding Judaica collection; in the formation of a marvellous school - the United Synagogue Day School - to disseminate Jewish learning, and also of Camp Ramah as a facility for Jewish living for the young.

The miracle of Stuart Rosenberg was "Bezalel": his standing in God's own shadow; for when the flight of his creative intuition was completed, when his vision had materialized and taken shape, the outcome was not just a brilliant individualistic exercise of innovative virtuosity. It was the authentic realization of what God had meant. His creation was true to the divine matrix.

Thus, this great, uniquely gifted man was a powerful and beneficial influence in our community. His life was dedicated to authentic Judaism, to scholarship, to Zionism and the State of Israel, to the Synagogue and to individual responsibility for the welfare of the community. He contributed to Jewish unity as a founder of the Toronto Rabbinic fellowship.

With awe and admiration we pay tribute to the man and his achievements.

Of Power Peacefully Surrendered

Politically I am eclectic. I am not committed to any political party. My allegiance, or partisan preference, shifts easily from one party to the other depending on the issues at hand. Often my views straddle the party lines: I agree with the position of one party on certain issues and disagree on others. My vote in an election is usually determined by my opinion of the candidates.

At the same time, I know that the welfare of our society depends on the political process. Political power has a profound impact on our community and on all levels of the public.

For this reason, I have a lively interest in politics and a deep respect and admiration for politicians. I know it is fashionable, and occasionally justified, to belittle politicians, to disparage their motivations and criticize their efforts. Yet I cling to the belief that most men and women in politics want to be genuine servants of the public. It takes a great deal of idealism to enter and remain in politics. If egotistical motivations and self-serving ambitions have launched many political careers, the same may be said of many other community leaders, professionals or volunteers, not excluding members of the rabbinate or of the religious ministry in general.

I have always enjoyed my personal contacts with political figures. I was very happy, therefore, when I was asked to participate at the swearing-in ceremony of David Peterson as Premier of Ontario and of his cabinet by offering a prayer. The fact that it was the first transfer of power from one party to another in forty years added excitement to the occasion.

As always, the global background of the ceremony was one of turmoil and political upheaval in many parts of the world. The contrast between the peaceful transition of power in Ontario and the violence marking political change in other lands was striking. Regardless of partisan loyalty, the people of Ontario had reasons to be thankful.

My prayer reflected that feeling.

Of Power Peacefully Surrendered ――――――
A Prayer at the Swearing-in Ceremony of Premier David Peterson and the Cabinet of the Province of Ontario June 26, 1985 at Queen's Park, Toronto

*A*lmighty God,

Yours is kingship and power. In your wisdom, you have challenged us with the management of our collective lives and charged us with the responsibility of exercising lawful authority and just government. Prayerfully, we ask for your blessings on the Premier-Designate, David Peterson, of the Province of Ontario, and the members of his cabinet as they are about to take the oath of their office.

How grateful we are to live in this blessed democracy Canada, and particularly in this beautiful province of Ontario, which for decades now has pointed the way to the creation of a benign, harmonious, egalitarian and pluralistic society. As governmental power passes from one political party to another, we give thanks for the democratic freedom embodied in this transition. How good it is to live in a land where political power is peacefully surrendered; where politicians try to defeat their opponents, but not to destroy them; where they contend honourably, respectfully and collegially, separated by differences of political ideology but united by common loyalty to our political system and to the interests of the people.

Deeper than the disappointment of defeat, and stronger than the exultation of victory, must be our shared joy in this triumph of democratic government. It is the victory of every party and of all people. May this hour, o God, be for all of us a time of thanksgiving for our precious freedom and of our reconsecration to the service of our community. Amen.

Change: Calamity or Challenge?

Change has been a part of my life, as it has for most of us.

Some changes were inward, relating to my intellectual and spiritual growth. I am not the same person in terms of my philosophy of life, my "Weltanschauung," my theological beliefs, my interpretation of Judaism, my emotional susceptibility and many other character traits, as I was at age eighteen. These changes were brought about by the influences of teachers and friends, books and colleagues, as well as by my own thinking and intellectual ferment. The Jewish Seminary in Würzburg, Germany, the Yeshiva in London, England, my revered teacher Rabbi Abraham A. Price, who ordained me at the Yeshiva in Toronto, my years as student and faculty member at the University of Toronto - all left their mark on my development and changed the direction of my thought, my faith and my intellectual opinions. These changes were sometimes far-reaching, decisive and difficult, but they were inner changes and lacked the trauma of change imposed by outside force.

However, there was also painful, wrenching change in the course of my life. The first occurred on the fateful January 30th, 1933, when Hitler and the National-Socialist Party of Germany took power, an event that turned me from a young and high-minded German and Jewish twelve-year-old child into a persecuted and despised subhuman outsider in the very world I had considered to be mine.

My emigration from Germany, in January 1939, was again a turning point, at which the Jewish teenager became a refugee.

My involuntary, accidental migration to Canada produced yet another change in my status, albeit an auspicious one. Few changes could be more radical than marriage and parenthood, happy events though they be.

Ordination and the start of a Rabbinical career brought change of a different sort. It tied my personal life to changes occurring in my congregation as it developed from a small parochial downtown congregation to a suburban community of 1,900 families.

*The greatest change I experienced in very recent time was my retire-
ment. I know that for many people, retirement is traumatic. I was fortunate
in that several important circumstances, both private and official, facilitated the transition for me, thus minimizing the shock.*

Nevertheless, retirement is a profound change.

*Furthermore, the fact that I had been the "spiritual leader" of my con-
gregation for 42 years and was expected to remain associated with it as
"Rabbi Emeritus" gave my retirement a particular coloration. It made me
very conscious of a certain "noblesse oblige." I could not draw the veil
of discreet privacy around myself as I went through the experience. I felt
duty-bound, first of all, to try to set an example for my congregants in
negotiating the trials of a process which many of them would also have
to undergo at some time. Secondly, the experience of going through retirement in the public spotlight obligated me to share with the members of
my congregation the insights which the process had yielded to me.*

*I lost no time. My very first sermon as "Rabbi Emeritus," whose man-
date included participating in the High Holiday Services, dealt with the
problem of "Change."*

Is it a calamitous crisis, as some people fear, or is it a challenging opportunity?

Change: Calamity or Challenge? ———————
Preached on Rosh Hashana 5750 - 1989

"Shana Tova! - A Good Year!"

This is our greeting on "Rosh Hashana," the salutation by which
we bless one another on our New Year Festival.

"Shana" is an intriguing word. Did you know it was related to the
well-known phrase *"Ma Nishtana,"* the familiar Passover question
about this night being "different?" Shana is also related to the Hebrew
word for "two": "Shnayim" or "Shtayim."

The root word "shanah" is very versatile. Its basic meaning is "to
repeat." By derivation, it also came to mean "to learn," for we learn
by repetition. The *"Mishnah,"* another derivative of the root, is the
basic collection of Jewish law, a body of learning preserved by
repeated rehearsal of the content.

79

Yet the root "shanah" also has the very opposite meaning. It means "to change, to make something different." "*Shinnui*" is the name of a party in Israel dedicated to "Change." The reflexive mode of the verb yields the word "*nishtana*," meaning "changed, different"; hence the popular "*mah nishtana:*" "*why is this night 'changed' or 'different?'*"

Thus, the word "Shana" and the Festival of Rosh Hashana present us both with the ambiguity of repetition and change, and with a paradox of continuity and revolution.

Viewed superficially, each new year is a repetition of the old. No hiatus interrupts the monotonous continuum of time. Sunrise, sunset; month following month; another fall, another spring. Repetition of the past. Another pair of shoes, another dress. Another electricity bill, another Visa statement. Repetition; again and again.

However, time is also the vehicle of change.

How traumatic, incisive, and painful change can be! And some changes brought on by time are irreversible.

I once heard Rabbi Jack Riemer at a Sermon Seminar. He said: "A good sermon is about yourself. It must deal with your own problem."

Today, I confess, I am preaching about myself. I have just undergone one of the greatest changes of my life. I have entered "retirement."

Each of us must face up to change.

We enter a new school; we start a new job; we get married; we get -God forbid!- divorced. We confront new ways of doing things. We watch social and ethnic changes in our community. We move into a new house, or into an apartment or condominium after having lived for years in our own home. We become richer; we become poorer. We retire. Age changes our physique and triggers changes in the functioning of our bodies and minds. The state of our health changes.

It is often difficult to cope with such change.

Change comes in various forms which trigger different emotional syndromes.

Let me start with mine.

Yesterday, I was the chief rabbi of my congregation, the "mara d'atra," its Rabbinic authority. Today I have become Rabbi Emeritus: a nice honour, a prestigious position, but -I must face it- the title says I am a "has-been." Someone else has my job! Someone else sits in my seat, stands at my pulpit, works in the office I occupied for so many years. Someone else is doing what I would do if I were still alive!

What did I say? If I were still *alive*?

Exactly. In this kind of change it is as if you were seeing the world after your own death.

You may supply other examples of this type of change.

You lost your girl friend. There she walks down the street holding someone else's hand, as if you no longer existed!

The trauma of divorce has similar aspects, and so do many kinds of change in which the world goes on without you. You are, literally, without.

The second type of change is the death of your world while you survive.

You worked for a company for 25 years. It goes out of business. The office that was like your own home is no longer there.

You are an expert on the manufacture of a certain product. Suddenly, as a result of technological change, there is no longer a market for your product. Your world is dead; yet you remain alive.

There is the "empty-nest syndrome." Your life has revolved around your home and your children. You have served breakfasts and made sandwiches. Suddenly, these things -or is it you?- are no longer needed.

A spouse dies. Whether death occurs suddenly, or whether the survivor had been burdened for a long period with the care for the spouse, when death occurs there ensues a serious dislocation. The survivor no longer feels needed. The world has vanished with the spouse.

Another type of change is being a stranger in a new land.

A new immigrant experiences the trauma of this type. He is surrounded by people speaking a strange language and practising foreign customs. "I used to be able to read street signs," he wonders, "I was able to understand the radio announcer. Now I am a dummy!"

A student entering a new school, a worker starting a new job, a newly married bride or groom, a family moving into a new neighbourhood - all these are instances of this type of change: the perplexity of unfamiliar circumstances, the bewilderment of new surroundings.

Future shock is another example of the same type of change. We find it difficult to adjust to technological changes, to adapt to new methods of doing things. The ubiquitous use of computers presented a scary puzzle for many people.

Change induces fear.

We are afraid of change. Change makes us fear the future.

How can we cope?

Rosh Hashana -the New Year- teaches us how to cope with change.

Rosh Hashana is the birthday of the world in our liturgy. *"Ha-yom harat olam - Today the world was born"* (Mahzor).

One of the central figures of our prayers is Isaac who was nearly sacrificed when God tested his father Abraham's obedience.

Isaac exemplified the first type of change: surviving one's own death, almost. The world continues while we are thrust out.

Rosh Hashana dares us to change. It calls for "Teshuva": radical reformation, a complete change of direction!

Usually, change is forced on us by circumstances. Rosh Hashana counters with the proposition that change ought to come from within ourselves. The idea of Teshuva is that we can initiate change. To cope with change enforced from the outside we must make it the occasion for an inner change, for self-created change.

Be not a victim of change, but become its author! Think of change as a God-given challenge for self-renewal.

Above all, do not fear change but welcome it! Change is exciting. It is a new opportunity to grow. It is a gateway to a wonderful new adventure.

The first day in school is a traumatic passage from a protective world to a competitive one. A child may stand crying at the classroom door but what he is so terrified to enter is not really a realm of danger and terror but a marvellous world of excitement and learning.

The new immigrant, so lonely and strange, stands on the threshold of great opportunities.

The fear that clutches the heart of the bride or the groom will quickly melt in the intimacy of a shared life and in the positive experience of becoming a family.

Change is liberating. It frees you from the shackles of the past. You no longer carry some of the old burdens.

In thinking of my retirement, I do not dwell on the authority I had to give up, but on the weight of responsibility from which I was relieved. Indeed, I delight in my liberation.

Having moved into a condominium, you may miss the feeling of independence you used to enjoy in a home of your own. Think of your freedom from snow removal instead!

Your nest is empty? Do not grieve! You may be able to reduce your economic responsibilities in favour of other pursuits. You are at leisure to travel more than in the past. You have a chance perhaps to go back to school to resume a field of study you had to abandon earlier in life. You are now free to help other people.

Always emphasize what you stand to gain from change, not what you appear to lose!

You lost your job? It hurts, surely. Yet, on reviewing your plight, you may discover an opportunity of starting a new career, of beginning a new life, a new exciting challenge of your capabilities.

Does your retirement scare you? Does it feel like death, like the world carrying on without you? I remember a very fine gentleman, active in our congregation for many decades. Engaged in retail business, he was frustrated by his inability to attend Shabbat services regularly and deeply regretted it. Circumstances forced him to retire. He truly began a new life in which he became a pillar of our congregation, a veritable leader in our community, and was blessed with a long fruitful life.

We pray today *"l'takkein olam b'malchut shaddai - that we may repair and improve the world as the Kingdom of the Almighty."* Does it not mean to change the world and to change ourselves?

For change is redemptive!

To have a vision of a better world and then to change the existing world - is that not the essence of redemption? Is not redemption the ultimate, the complete change?

How, then, can we fear change?

So what is a "Shana Tova - A Good Year"?

"Shana Tova" means that when our world changes, we will respond by accepting the challenge, and thereby change ourselves. "Shana Tova" also means continuity which we shall find through trust in our God: *"For I am the Lord who does not change"* (Malachi 3:6). God remains the same: immutable and eternal, the constant source of our confidence, the firm root of our "Bitachon," our faith and trust. Believing in Him and sure of His love, we cannot be afraid, as we joyously affirm in the last line of "Adon Olam": *"God is with me, I have no fear!"* Amen.

Der Tag der Kirche: My Challenge to German Christians

How I became involved with Christian churches in Germany is described in the fourth section of this book. [1]

My involvement culminated in my acceptance of an invitation to be the keynote speaker on October 31, 1988, at the "Day of the Church," a yearly rally of Protestants in celebration of the "Reformation Festival."

The invitation itself was historic. It was the first time ever that a non-Christian had been asked to address this annual gathering of several thousand Christians in Cologne, the city of my birth. The proposal to invite me, when first made, was not approved without lengthy controversy. Even some of my German friends, whose motivation was definitely not tainted by anti-Jewish feelings, questioned sincerely and strongly the propriety and the rationale of asking a Jew to address a rally that is intended primarily to strengthen the bonds between the Church and its followers.

However, the proponents of the idea prevailed. The proximity of the rally date to the fiftieth anniversary of "Crystal Night" was persuasive. Crystal Night - November 10th, 1938 - was the night when in Germany hundreds of Synagogues were incinerated, Jewish homes and businesses invaded and trashed, and thousands of Jews arrested and taken to Concentration Camps. Eighteen years old at the time, I was among those incarcerated in Dachau. In commemoration of the fiftieth anniversary, which was prominently observed all over Germany, I, a Jew, was invited to come from Canada to speak to Christians on a Christian theme from a Jewish and personal perspective.

The theme, which reads better in German than in English, was "God Liberates and Grants Atonement: Together on the Road to the Future."

My emotions that night were heightened by the circumstance that I spoke in a convention centre located not far from my erstwhile parental home, in an area familiar to me as a youth. I did not know when I spoke that it had been also the assembly point from which my parents and sister, together with thousands of other Cologne Jews, had been deported to the ghetto of Riga.

I was able to convey my emotional turbulence to my listeners who were spellbound by the encounter with a Jew, a Rabbi, born in Cologne, having come back to speak to Christians on themes both searching and painful. For me, despite my inner conflicts, it was one of the highlights of my career as a teacher of Judaism.

All the same, I was awed by the deep impression my words made and by the chain reaction they started.

I spoke in German. I had lost my fluency in German long ago, but I had made an intensive effort to regain sufficient command of my mother tongue to be effective. I had gone into seclusion for a few days while I prepared my address surrounded by German books and dictionaries at a cottage on Lake Simcoe.

The text presented here is my own English translation of the original with slight editorial emendations for the benefit of my English-speaking readers.

Der Tag der Kirche: My Challenge to German Christians ——————————
An address in Cologne, Germany, at the Annual Day of the Church on October 31, 1988

The Temple was destroyed; Jerusalem lay in ruins.

When the Rabbis who had escaped death or deportation at the hands of the Romans regrouped in the little town of Yavneh to resume studying and teaching, they searched for the proper preamble to their first lessons. Most of the Sages, it is reported, introduced their discourses with an expression of gratitude and praise for the hospitality of the townspeople who had offered asylum for the Torah and its teachers.

Following this tradition, I would like to extend to you, Ladies and Gentlemen, my sincere thanks for the invitation to address you. I highly appreciate the friendly reception that you have given me.

I am deeply moved by the opportunity afforded me tonight to make a contribution to the religious and spiritual life of the city of my birth.

Yet I do not stand before you as a son of Cologne, driven out long ago and now invited back. I am addressing you as a Jew and as a representative of the Jewish people.

Dialogue between Germans and Jews is a very problematic, delicate and often painful process. Loaded down with the heavy baggage we carry, we cannot find it easy to surmount the obstacles. The tragedy of the past deprives us of the ability to speak.

Nevertheless!

Difficult as it may be for Germans and Jews to converse, Jews and Christians, even German Christians, share a common language. When we relate to one another as members of kindred religious traditions, we see a flicker of hope: *God liberates and grants atonement.*

But we must start at the beginning.

In February of 1941, a German soldier, Joe Heydecker, was able to take hundreds of photographs of the Warsaw Ghetto. They were published in book form in 1983.

Last summer I spent a few weeks in Israel. As I usually do, I subjected my feelings to the trauma of a visit to the Holocaust Museum, Yad Vashem, opening anew old wounds deep in my heart. I visited a new building, dedicated to the memory of the million and a half children who perished in the Holocaust. Finally, I walked into an exhibit of Holocaust art and there I saw a number of Warsaw Ghetto photographs. They broke my heart.

The pictures of starving children began to obsess me.

"Heart-rending," Heydecker calls their plight in his book. "Most of them were covered in rags, squatting, lying or sleeping on the side of the street, whimpering, begging in vain for a hand-out, their feet wrapped in old sacks, eyes hollow with hunger, without shelter from the cold."

Among the pictures I saw was one of a young child trying to feed

87

a younger sibling; I saw pictures of children dying on the ground and of others already dead, waiting for the daily collection of corpses.

One thought haunts me like a demon. Before they drew the last breath of their miserable lives, how did these children construe the meaning of this world? What was their view of life? Could they regard the world as anything but a place of horror, holding but misery, suffering and cruelty? Could they find a meaning in life, in that hell of pain, torture and despair?

When my parents, deported from Cologne in 1941, perished in the Riga Ghetto or in a death camp near-by, at the ages of 57 and 55 years, they knew at least that in this world of ours there exists not only evil, but also good; that there is also love and that somewhere justice may be found. But these poor children knew nothing! They experienced only evil, only fear, only rage and death. Did their world have any room for a deity? The idea of a loving God must have been beyond their grasp. If there was a god, he would have to be -I hesitate to utter the words- a satanic monster!

This view of the world must be our starting point. It is the deepest spiritual darkness, our heaviest burden.

This is the world that drove out God.

This is the world that cries out for liberation and atonement.

Is there still time? Is it not yet too late? Did the world not already lose its soul in the Warsaw Ghetto? Was this soul not burned at Auschwitz, so that there is nothing left but a soulless automaton, an empty shell of a world? Is mankind not spinning in a downward spiral of doom to an apocalyptic crash as a hopeless, failed experiment of nature - or a cosmic joke which the creator has allowed himself?

Our religious traditions try to convince us that the human condition is never hopeless. True, we can frustrate God's design, they suggest, but only for a time, never for all eternity.

God's own essence is our guarantee. Isaiah said it:

> *Do you not know? Have you not heard? Our Lord is an eternal God ... He neither grows faint nor weary.. He gives strength to the tired, fresh vigour to the spent.* (40:28f)

Our eternal God never gives up! At Mount Sinai, our Lord introduced himself not as the creator, but as the liberator. He is the one who by liberating us from Egypt showed that he can pull us out of the deepest quagmire. He never grows tired. He neither despairs nor resigns. He gives us new chances, again and again.

However, it is not entirely up to God. In Jewish theology we find the doctrine, possibly in the main stream of Jewish thought, that we human beings have the responsibility for making redemption possible and keeping its possibility alive. To liberate ourselves from guilt, to overcome the past, is *our* challenge, not God's. We ourselves must discover and make ready the means of redemption.

Redemption is not the negation, the wiping out, of human history, but its fulfilment. It is we who must start the process, clean up our world and pave the highway of redemption.

While we are waiting for the Messiah, the Messiah is waiting for us!

Do not rely on a Messiah to save you from your own responsibility, to simply clean off the slate of the past and to offer atonement for all your guilt without an inner turning and a drastic revision of your conduct!

Our faith in redemption gives us the assurance that the cosmos is not neutral; that God helps and encourages us and that he is waiting for us. The Midrash on the Song of Songs (5:2) quotes God as saying, *"My children, make for me an opening of Repentance be it as small as a needle's eye, and I will make for you an opening through which wagons and carriages can pass."*

But we must make the opening.

If it is up to us to take the first step; if our repentance and reformation is the prerequisite of redemption, then we cannot evade the need to examine the past and to understand it.

What went wrong?

How was it possible that in November 1938 Christian hands put hundreds of Synagogues to the torch, trashed and looted thousands of Jewish homes, stores and schools? How could the Church tolerate in silence the annihilation of millions of Jews? How could a so-called Christian people acquiesce in all these outrages and fail to rise up in indignation?

The first murder in Biblical history was fratricide. *"Where is your brother Abel?"* God asked the murderer. We all know Cain's answer: *"I do not know. Am I my brother's keeper?"* (Genesis 4:9).

Right here we get to the essence of the story. First, the old yet always convenient alibi: "I did not know anything! We knew nothing at all! We did not see anything!"

The murderer denies the deed and the knowledge thereof.

The second sentence goes right to the heart of the matter. The murderer asks a rhetorical question. "Am I my brother's keeper?"

"No," Cain is saying, "I am not responsible for him. He is not my concern. It's none of my business."

In the course of the millennia we have learned a little better, I believe. Yes, we are responsible. We are our brother's keeper. What we have not yet learned is the answer to a closely related question:

"Who is my brother?"

For my brother, no sacrifice is too great. For my brother, I will do everything, even hazard my own life. But only for my brother - and you, and you and you, you are not my brothers! You are Frenchmen, Jews, Catholics, Turks!

How can we tolerate children starving to death in Africa? Because we do not really feel that they are our brothers and sisters.

How can we sleep peacefully when thousands are drowned by floods in Bangladesh? They are not our brothers, that's why.

We have split humanity into pieces.

In the Talmudic tractate Sanhedrin, the ancient rabbis posed a fundamental question. Why did God create only one human being? Why not a white man, and a black and a yellow and a red?

They give two apparently independent answers.

The first: God created one Adam only so that no human may boast "My ancestor was greater than yours!" Since we all are descendants of the same pair of ancestors, we are of equal nobility. Thus, human equality, the equal value of all human beings, becomes a basic principle in the divine plan of creation.

The second answer is that God wanted to demonstrate his glorious power. When a king issues coins bearing his portrait, they will all be identical, since they are minted in the same mould. Our King Most High, our divine creator, made us all in the mould of his own image. Yet you will not find two identical persons in the whole world! Thus, God's glory is the variety of human beings, their many splendoured diversity.

The two answers to the question of monogenesis, why God created one Adam only, are not alternatives. They are interlinked.

Our Sages wanted to reconcile equality and diversity. The infinite variety of individuals does not insinuate different grades of value. To the contrary. Sameness diminishes value. Because we are each unique and different, we are of equal worth. It is precisely our variety that gives us equivalence.

Clearly, this Talmudic passage addresses itself to pluralism.

We must accept positively the fact that humanity, although it is one, is composed of different groups and types. We must be open to the idea, therefore, that while God is one, more than one way may lead him.

Pluralism has special significance for Christian-Jewish relations.

The Christian Church has always considered itself as the successor of the Jewish people. By not accepting the Redeemer offered to them, the Jews broke their covenant with God and lost their status as God's chosen people. Christendom is now the true Israel. Rejected by God, despised by Christians, the Jewish people are forced to bear witness to the truth of this theological thesis by suffering their painful fate. Good Christians will not approve or abet the physical annihilation of the Jews, but they know how to rationalize it.

In this manner, the Church has preserved a built-in anti-Semitism which facilitates or at least explains the cruel persecutions of Jews. It enabled Christians to remain passive and thus make the Holocaust possible.

The Talmudic teachers ask what the quarrel between Cain and Abel was about. What dispute could have aroused such passion as to lead to the slaying of a brother?

One answer is especially poignant for us: Cain and Abel argued about the location of the Holy Temple. Each insisted that the temple was to be built in his territory.

The provocation for the murder was a quarrel over religious truth. Whose is the true religion?

As long as this exclusivist attitude persists, the prospect of meaningful relations between Jews and Christians, and of a future they can share together, remains dim.

Let us think! Do we not diminish the power of divinity, the greatness of our God, if we impose limitations on him and prescribe for him that he is allowed to acknowledge only one religion as true; that he may only consider one community as exclusively his own?

We human beings have no difficulty reconciling several loyalties. I can be true at the same time to parents, children and a spouse; I can be a loyal Jew and a loyal Canadian. Why should God then be restricted to one loyalty only?

May God not enter a covenant with more than one partner? May God not delight in the unquestioning commitment of one Church without disowning the more analytical approach of another as false? May God not love Christendom as his people without dismissing the people Israel? Must we, like Cain and Abel, degrade and scorn one another, branding every faith save ours as falsehood, in order to validate the truth of our own belief?

Can we be so absolutely certain that only we are God's chosen? Can anyone?

The prophets warn us against the deceptive conceit of an exclusive relationship to God. *"Are you not just like the Ethiopians to me, o people Israel?"* (Amos 9:7). And the prophet Isaiah, speaking God's words, said: *"Blessed be my people Egypt and Assyria, the work of my hands, and Israel, my heritage!"* (Isaiah 19:25).

No one group, no single religion, has an exclusive relationship to the Sovereign of the universe. No one in this perplexed and perplexing world may claim to possess absolute truth. All we may do is confess our own faith and proclaim our commitment to search for God and for truth.

And we must accord others the same right.

The Jewish people cannot claim an exclusive chosenness. Others may also be chosen. Christianity cannot claim to be the only valid and efficacious means of salvation for all humanity.

And all of us must be prepared to be judged by our deeds. How much love, goodness, compassion, humility and sacrifice has our faith produced in its adherents? This is the only reliable measurement of human truth.

92

Once, a man was lost in a dark forest. For many hours he wandered searching for a way out. In vain! Desperation seized him as the darkness of night descended. Suddenly, he saw a light in the far distance which slowly came closer and closer: a man carrying a lantern!

With profound relief he ran toward him.

"Thanks heaven, I found you!" he cried out. "Now you will show me the way out of the forest!"

"I am sorry," replied the other, "but I am lost just like you and I have been wandering through this forest for a long time seeking an exit. But one thing I can tell you for certain: the way I came is not the right way! And now let us search for the right way together!"

This certainty we also have: the way we came was not the right way. The road of exclusivity, the way of validating our status by denying the validity of others was a road that led to fragmentation, to hatred, to cruelty, to genocide.

The way we came was the way of error and insanity. Misled, we blundered into a world which to this day permits tribes in Africa to exterminate one another. We got lost in a world in which the profit motive is stronger than our responsibility for the environment, with the result that we pass on to our children polluted rivers and poisoned air. The way we came took us through a period in which a shaky world peace could be maintained only through the extortionist threat of nuclear global annihilation.

If we learn to think in pluralistic terms, then humanity may become one brotherhood. If we are free to relish our multi-coloured variety, then we will be able to live in unity and harmony. By defending diversity, the right to be different, we defend the oneness and the equal value of all human beings. Through pluralism we become brothers. So we must look for the right way together. The road to the future is the road wide enough for all.

The road we can share will take us into a future in which we shall accept responsibility for the protection of nature and for the preservation of the environment. The world shall be our sacred trust.

In our future together, we shall share our bread with the hungry and realize that a starving child defaces our divine image.

In our future together, world peace will grow out of the consciousness that we are all really sisters and brothers, each one of us irreplaceable in the love of our heavenly father.

Let us start then on our Messianic agenda! Our God, who offers liberation, redemption and atonement, is waiting for us! We must not keep him waiting any longer. The world cannot afford it.

So let us raise the lantern, join hands, and look together for the new way, the way into our common future!

---

1   *See Introduction to "To Canada with Love," page 147*

The THIRD *window*

Liberate Your Soul!

Self-imposed slavery is a rampant scourge.

The sermon "Liberate Your Soul!" was not triggered by any particular incident. As Rabbi, I have always known people whose problems were caused by the conflict between their spiritual needs and their bondage to their perceived responsibilities.

The promise of creative leisure made by modern technology has not been fulfilled. We are surrounded by the ubiquitous evidence of self-imposed slavery which deprives people of the freedom indispensable to their humanity.

"Liberate Your Soul!" has a double meaning. It refers not only to the emancipation of the inner self, but also to the rehabilitation of a simple spiritual concept that has been displaced in our modern understanding of ourselves: the human soul. Old-fashioned, imprecise, poetic, the idea of a soul has been steam-rollered by the weight of modern realism and the impact of contemporary psychology.

In my sermon I aimed at encouraging people at Passover time, when freedom is high on our spiritual agenda, to liberate themselves from the bondage of the modern lifestyle. I also intended to revive the notion of a "soul" and restore it to a position of respect in the inventory of ideas by which we try to shape our lives.

Liberate Your Soul! _____
Preached on the eighth Day of Passover 5746 - 1986

The Exodus from Egypt is mentioned no less than fifty times in the Torah. The number reflects its pervasive impact on the consciousness of Israel and on the Jewish ethos.

"Why precisely fifty times?" the ancient commentators ask.

The number fifty recalls the Year of the Jubilee. Observed every fifty years, the Jubilee was the year in which all slaves were to be set free.

Slavery, ubiquitous in antiquity and still surviving in some enclaves of the Third World, existed also in ancient Israel. Its forms were relatively humane, but the Torah allows an indigent individual to enter slavery as a means of repaying his debts and it provides for thieves to be forced into bondage in order to make restitution. After a maximum of seven years, the indentured servant had the option of release from service. Even if he declined, the Year of Jubilee terminated his servitude.

In the course of history, slavery was abolished. Today, we are all free.

"Thank God, I am not a slave!" we say every morning in our prayers. There are no more slaves.

"No more slaves? You must be kidding, Rabbi!"

"Ask some housewives, bonded to the kitchen, servants to their children, consorts to husbands, drafted as chauffeurs, working as domestics, plumbers, gardeners without wages; marketing, repairing, and perhaps holding a part-time outside job as well!"

"Ask some men, whether slavery has been abolished, and they will tell you about all-consuming jobs, merciless business obligations, unceasing commitments, demanding clients, hard-driving bosses, impossible pressures and endless hours."

And ask your divine soul, your "Neshama," that ineffable self, the mysterious core of your personality, your innermost heart, the essence that makes you human and God's child. Ask that soul of yours whether there is slavery, bondage, servitude!

What I call soul is not the "Life Force." The Life Force is called

Family

The first picture
with mother – *1920*

With parents and brother on a
Sunday outing – *1923*

Schild as student in London,
England – *1939*

The last
family portrait,
January 1939

*After Dachau, the
family sat for what
they rightly feared
would be their last
picture together:
Hermann and Hetti
Schild, brother Kurt
and sister Margot*

War and Destruction

above left:
The house after an air
raid – *ca. 1942*

above right:
The Schild family
home on a picture
postcard – *ca. 1901*

The house in ruin after the end of
the war – *1945*
*Picture taken by author's uncle who
survived in hiding in Amsterdam .*

The historic synagogue in
Cologne-Mulheim where
Schild family worshipped.

First burned by the Nazis during
"Crystal Night" November 10, 1938,
the synagogue was further destroyed
by allied bombers. Today, a plaque is
the only trace.

The Pathway to Learning

Senior high school year
in Cologne – *1937*
*Schild obtained special
permission to attend despite
general ban on Jewish students.*

Elementary School in Mulheim:
Second Grade – *1927*
Schild in 3rd row, 2nd from right

*With another Jew, he is
confined to back row.*

"Were not your
Torah my delight
I would have
perished in my
affliction"
(Psalm 119:92).

Torah study
in Canadian
Internment –
*Camp I, Fort Lennox,
Que. – 1941*

Yeshiva Torath Chaim, Toronto
Students with Dean, Rabbi Abraham A. Price – *1943*

Ordination at
Yeshiva Torath
Chaim – 1947

Front row (R. to L.):
Rabbi Isaac Stollman,
Rabbi Joshua
Hershorn, Rabbi
Abraham A. Price.
Standing (R. to L.):
Mr. Joseph Osolke,
newly ordained rabbis
Joel Litke, Albert
Pappenheim,
Erwin Schild.

Degrees and Dedication

Bachelor of Arts 1947
(Oriental Languages),
University of Toronto

above:
Doctor of Divinity h.c.,
Jewish Theological Seminary,
New York, 1975 – with Chancellor
Gerson D. Cohen

Left:
Dedication of new Adath
Israel Synagogue Building 1959 –
with Lieut. Governor
John Keiller Mackay

"Nefesh" in Hebrew. We share it with the animals. It is the force that has to do with self-preservation.

What I call "Neshama," soul, is the opposite of the animalistic life force. The Neshama enables us to sacrifice life rather than try to preserve it. When self-preservation would mandate otherwise, the Neshama enables a parent to run into a burning house to save a child and a soldier to retrieve a wounded comrade under fire.

Our soul enables us to bear calamity through faith. It enables us to speak to God in prayer when logic would brand prayer as foolish. It enables us to believe in God and to know he is near even when our experience seems to bear out the opposite.

The "Neshama" is what goads us to learn, to expand our knowledge; not just what we must know for material gain but to explore the Unknown and to speculate about what cannot even be explored. "Neshama" is the source of our divine curiosity.

The "Neshama" teaches us what is good, right and just — not merely what is useful, expedient and profitable. Our conscience is the voice of our soul.

Our noblest emotions have to do with our soul, emotions we are sometimes embarrassed to entertain, preferring instead to acknowledge only those feelings that derive from our physical nature, such as hunger, lust, greed, and sensual pleasure.

Yet we are capable of noble feelings that originate in the "Neshama." We are able to produce a painting or to be moved by one. We can compose a symphony or be transported by music, by words or by poetry. These qualitites have to do with our "Neshama."

We have the ability to love. We are able to adopt another human being as part of ourselves. We are able to be a companion to someone; we may take a walk with someone and, as if by magic, it turns into a new experience. We can share with others and thus make our portion bigger. We can share a movie, an idea, a worry, a sorrow. In all these relationships, our "Neshama" is at work.

Alas, our precious "Neshama" may become enslaved and suppressed!

We have to work, hour upon hour, day upon day, without pause.

We have commitments: families, mortgages, chalets, careers.

We must keep up with our friends who have sumptuous homes, boats and condos in far-away places.

We have to meet or beat the competition. Like the Hebrews in ancient Egypt, we have taskmasters over ourselves: bosses, bank managers, shareholders, husbands, wives, and children who need and want.

And so, the "Neshama" becomes enslaved and groans under the burden, as did the Israelite slaves in bondage, and, like the Israelites, the soul cries out to God for release.

There are suggestions of liberation.

We hear voices: "You work too hard!" "Take it easy!" "*Shallach et ammi - let my people go!*" (Exodus 5:2).

"Read a good book! Go to Synagogue! Observe Shabbat - the day of the 'Neshama,' the day of 're-creation.' Make time for a concert, a play, a good movie! When was the last time you went to a museum and looked leisurely at a display, opening windows for your soul? Do some 'Mitzvot' to give your soul a respite from bondage!"

But Pharaoh stubbornly refuses. What did the King of Egypt say? "You are lazy!. You don't work hard enough! '*tichbad ha'avoda - work harder!'"* (Exodus 5:9). We need more money, more pleasures, more things, more pressures! We're reaching the top - so let's work a little extra! Cut out a little more spare time... the half-hour with the kids... the Friday evening with the family.

And then, as we keep refusing to set the "Neshama" free, there come the TEN PLAGUES:

HYPERTENSION,

DEPRESSION,

SKIN DISEASE,

BURN-OUT,

ALCOHOLISM,

DRUG DEPENDENCY,

NEUROSES,

ULCERS,

INTESTINAL DISEASE,

HEART ATTACK.

100

Like Pharaoh who yielded and repented under the impact of each plague only to change his mind when the plague stopped, so we also promise to reform and change our ways while the plague is upon us.

How often have I stood at the bedside of a stricken patient and heard the words "Rabbi, if God only lets me live, I'll live differently! I shall work less, take off more time. You'll see me in Shul every Shabbat!"

You know the rest. The plague is removed, and the slavery of the soul resumes.

Let my people go. Grant your "Neshama" a little freedom.

Inevitably, there will be an ultimate Exodus. We are mortal. Eventually, the soul will be liberated from bondage. That is why we are holding "Hazkarat Neshamot" today: "Remembering the Souls." It is the *souls* we remember - not Dad's factory or Mom's white convertible. We recall souls, not bodies, houses, or material assets.

So don't let your soul wait for the final exodus. Liberate it now, while the breath of life is still within you!

Remember, at the core of your being there is something divine. Let it flourish. Sustain it with Torah; nourish it with Mitzvot; quicken it with prayer; refresh it weekly with Shabbat; renew it with the observance of the Festivals; protect it with Kashrut; enrich it with compassion for others and guard it with modesty.

And may God deem us worthy for the fulfilment of his promise (Exodus 15:26): *"Every disease that I inflicted on Egypt I shall not inflict on you, for I the Lord am your physician."*

Until Messiah Comes

To procrastinate is human. I am prone to put off some things because they are inconvenient, and others because more urgent business usurps my immediate attention.

There were times when I postponed a sermon. Something inhibited me from expressing my thoughts in public. Perhaps, I was not at peace with conclusions that collided with long-cherished beliefs or principles of mine. My conclusions may have been contrary to established Jewish positions or traditions. Why undermine traditional beliefs with which my congregants are comfortable, just because they run counter to a new insight of my own? Perhaps my thinking is not yet complete. Better to keep the pot simmering a little while longer on the back burner and examine the results at a future time!

An article which I read in "Commentary" magazine so many years ago that I remember neither the author's name nor the year of publication has helped me examine a problem that has troubled me for a long time.

What is the relationship between history and morality? Should we suspend moral judgement when historical events unfold and when the currents of change seem impervious to our sense of right and wrong?

With some misgivings, I finally decided to present my answer to this question in a sermon. I received the bonus of an idea that occurred to me: how to define the difference between historical time and the Messianic era. Since many people, both Jews and non-Jews, sense the approach of a new era, I found this insight so intriguing that I changed the title of my sermon from "History and Ethics" to "Until Messiah Comes."

Until Messiah Comes ──────────────

A Sermon on History and Ethics preached on the Second Day of Rosh Hashana 5751 - 1990

*I*s History moral?

This is a question with which I have wrestled for a long time. Can we, or indeed should we, apply the norms of morality, of right and wrong, to historical events of the past and to historical changes transpiring at the present time?

A little bird flies into a window pane. A child finds the bird with its wing broken, unable to fly, and nurses it back to health, till one day, the little bird flies away.

This is a lovely story for children. It exemplifies and teaches moral values: the virtue of compassion, the duty of helping the weak and the unselfishness of true goodness, for in the end the bird flies away.

No year is complete in Canada without a Whale Story. A whale has been beached, for example, and people help the animal out to sea. Last year, Television News brought us a running account of frantic efforts to rescue a number of whales trapped by ice. The whole country, drawing satisfaction from this act of public morality, was cheering for the volunteers who tried to cut a channel to the open sea, and many were dismayed when one of the whales did not make it.

If there is a Mother Nature, she would laugh. In nature's scheme one does not care about the irrelevant fate of one single whale or one bird. Nature is concerned with the survival and balance of the species, but utterly indifferent to the life or death of the individual.

If you have watched nature films, you must have seen a lion pouncing on a gazelle, or a falcon swooping down on a hapless field mouse. It is a brutal, but perfectly normal spectacle of nature. Should we in the name of morality try to convert lions to vegetarianism? In the context of nature, the fate of the individual is immaterial.

Human ethics is the opposite. It is our human burden to care for the individual, even the old, the sick or the weak - in fact, for all those whose survival is anything but a biological necessity.

Our government may spend thousands of dollars to find a hiker lost in the woods. We employ every resource to help even a single individual to survive. That is the glory of human morality.

Nature is amoral. Morality does not apply to it.

How about history?

Since human beings make history, should we expect that history abides by the canon of human ethics? Should we evaluate history in moral terms? Since history is the result of human activity, must it respect moral values such as human life and ownership?

Or is history more like nature? Is it perhaps part of nature, and therefore governed by rules that champion the survival of the species?

"What difference does it make?" you will ask.

If historical events must be evaluated in moral terms and the yardstick of ethics be applied to current historical developments, we are in trouble.

You have heard of the congregant who asked: "Rabbi, are we allowed to profit from the misfortune of someone else?"

"No; of course not!"

"Then please, would you mind giving me back the hundred dollars I paid you for my wedding ceremony?"

If history is subject to the critique of ethics, we must give this country back to the Mohawks, the Cree, the Hurons and the Inuit. European invaders stole this land, killed many of the owners and reduced survivors to pitiable conditions on reservations. If I inherit stolen goods, I am obligated to return them!

Must we go back whence our ancestors came?

Rosh Hashana is the anniversary of creation. *"Hayom harat olam - today is the birthday of the world"* (Mahzor).

Rashi's commentary on the Torah starts with a question:

Why does the Torah begin with the creation of the world? As a Law book, it should start with the first law!

The answer is startling:

> It is to justify Israel's possession of its land; for when
> the nations of the world will accuse Israel and say, "You

> *are thieves; you have stolen the land of the seven original*
> *nations," we can answer, "The whole world belongs to*
> *God, for He has created it; it was his will to give the*
> *land to the seven nations and his will to take it from*
> *them and to give it to us."*

What does that say?

Does it not say that historical processes do not obey the same rules of morality that regulate relations between individuals? What would be considered theft if committed by an individual, is the unfolding of a historical design authored by the Lord of History, God.

History then has a will of its own, a force, a thrust, a direction. Human beings, whether they be kings, generals, statesmen, soldiers or voters, play out a script that they did not write themselves. They are actors, not authors.

The notion of history having a will of its own would seem to contradict a fundamental Jewish teaching, the doctrine of moral causality.

Did the great Biblical prophets not proclaim the bold proposition that historical events have moral causes?

The prophets taught that a nation practicing injustice and oppression will suffer defeat and destruction. Not the strongest armies win the battle, but victory goes to the more righteous.

Does the Torah not remark at one point that the Israelites were allowed to conquer the Promised Land only because of wickedness of its former inhabitants?

Is that not contrary to my thesis?

Not at all. It really confirms my analysis.

Were all the Canaanites wicked at the time of the Israelite conquest so as to deserve to be dispossessed? Were there no good individuals who merited a better fate?

Were all Israelites corrupt when the prophets predicted their state would be destroyed and its inhabitants killed or exiled?

Is it just or moral to decree collective and indiscriminate punishment?

Abraham, the individual who is so closely associated with Rosh Hashana, pleads with God for justice when God is about to destroy the cities Sodom and Gemora. Maybe there are fifty, forty, ten righteous persons in the cities? You must be moral, he says to God. *"Shall the judge of the whole world not practice justice?"* (Genesis 18:25).

But Abraham has no qualms when God promises to his descendants the land of the Canaanites! He did not plead for the Canaanites as he did for the inhabitants of Sodom. Why not?

The answer is that the destruction of Sodom was God's work, and God must be moral. The conquest of Canaan was history, and different rules apply there.

Realistically, history has never been moral. Political history is the chronicle of war, conquest, exploitation and the displacement of one group by another. The Persians, Greeks, Romans, Goths, Arabs, Huns, Turks, Spaniards and British, each had their turn at conquest and dominion.

Did you notice how Rashi seems to anticipate the modern "double standard"?

The nations will accuse the Jews, says Rashi, of wresting their land from earlier inhabitants. "You are usurpers! You stole your land from the Canaanites."

Which nations are so righteous that they may level this accusation against the people Israel? Did they not do the very same thing?

Kings were expected to make wars and conquer, to squeeze tribute and taxes out of conquered territories, or to expel populations and settle their own people in their place.

The greatness of a ruler used to be measured by how many widows and orphans he made! What made Alexander "the Great," Catherine "the Great," Peter "the Great," and Frederick "the Great"?

Today the world champions oppressed Palestinians against their Israeli occupiers. If Jews had created their country a hundred years earlier, I doubt if anyone would have cared. Was it not just a century ago, when Britain, France and Germany were busy carving Africa and parts of Asia into colonies for themselves? Who cared what they did to the native populations of India or the Congo?

Why is this subject so important to me?

It is because I realize more and more that we must accept history for what it is and how it unfolds. We ought to stop blaming ourselves or the government of Israel for what may be an inexorable historical change. Perhaps we are needlessly agonizing and apologizing.

The founders of Israel, idealistic Zionist pioneers, wanted to live in peace side by side with the Arab population. They were prepared to share their techniques and resources, and for a long time they did.

Yet when the Jewish State became a reality, the Arabs responded with hostility, hatred and escalating attempts to demoralize and destroy Israel. The result of continued warfare and unrelenting terrorism has been a hardening of positions and growing intransigence. As far as its effect on Israelis is concerned, the Intifada was counterproductive. World opinion may have been deflected in a pro-Arab direction; but in Israel, it served to intensify hatred. Israeli countermeasures entrenched Arab hatred of Jews even more implacably and permanently.

"They hate us and we hate them." The hard line is gaining control.

I feel very uncertain of the outcome. I am beginning to despair of the possibility of peaceful accommodation. Perhaps there remains but a painful choice: either they or we. I want Israel to prevail - but that may have to be at the expense of the Arabs living in Israel or the territories and perhaps, even beyond.

It is important for me to understand that if this happens it will not mean that Israel's survival is founded on a breach of morality, any more than Americans or Canadians will regard the existence of the United States and Canada as the poisoned fruit of immorality.

Whatever may happen, whatever may become necessary to defend and secure the State of Israel, is for me the unfolding of a historical destiny - or of God's design - even if it cannot pass the test of the ethical standards we apply to our personal lives and dealings.

If Palestinians will have to put up with Jewish settlements in areas they want to be "judenrein;" if eventually numbers of Arabs will prefer to emigrate; if population exchanges or resettlements will be arranged or if the accumulated antagonism will preclude peaceful coexistence, do not charge Israel with immorality nor its policy with a disregard of Jewish ethics!

The highest ethical imperative of a government is to protect the interests of the people entrusted to it. The ethics of the individual call for the practice of self-denial and altruism. The moral person sacrifices his own interest for others. But that is individual morality, not the morality of government.

That is not an endorsement of cruelty, or of injustice deliberately inflicted on individuals. We don't have to give Canada back - but we must make sure that we treat the members of our native nations fairly and decently. We must take responsibility for their welfare and for their equality with all Canadians, not excluding their obligation to obey the law like all people in Canada. We must do everything possible to alleviate hardships for innocent people who are caught in the turning wheels of history; we must minimize personal suffering, ameliorate consequences and accept the widest measure of responsibility possible - in Israel as well as in Canada. Yet history must take its course. And it will.

Until the Mashiach will come and will bring history under the umbrella of ethics!

Did the prophet not promise that even Nature will accept moral norms in the Messianic Age when the lion will lie down with the lamb?

Even as a metaphor, that promise is meaningful. Indeed, it is an allegorical definition of the Messianic purpose: to reconcile history and morality, and to harmonize politics and ethics.

Which is what we mean when we pray on Rosh Hashana for God to become *"Melech al kol ha-aretz - King over all the earth"* - Amen!

Rome
or
Jerusalem

The growing threat of violence has been a characteristic mark of the last few decades.

Violence is utterly repugnant to the Jewish ethos. "The voice is Jacob's; the hands are Esau's!" - a quote from the Torah portion on which this sermon is based - has been a popular catch phrase to indicate how foreign violence is to the Jewish style.

I have used the theme of Jacob and Esau more than once to teach the Jewish abhorrence of violence. It is an important lesson at a time when violence, both in real life and as an over-exploited thrill-pandering spectacle in entertainment, continues to be on the rise.

For the State of Israel, forced to resort to military means to defend its existence, the corroding effect of violence is a tragic problem. All those who love her have faced this problem with fear and anguish. In 1984 no solution was yet in sight. Neither did we know how much more heart-wrenching the problem would become.

However, when cruel realities threaten to overwhelm the ideal, it is especially important to preserve the ideal in our minds.

Rome or Jerusalem
A Sermon preached on Shabbat Parshat
Toldot 5745 - 1984

Our personal safety, the quality of our lives, the integrity of the democratic political process and the stability of the international order are all jeopardized by one sinister threat: violence.

Worried parents must caution their children against the threat of malevolent adults. Police officers are being killed in Ontario and Quebec with frightening frequency. The Prime Minister of a populous democracy is assassinated [1] and the Prime Minister of the Mother of Democracies has but a narrow escape from the same fate. Terrorism has gained acceptance as an instrument of political change. A visiting Pope has to be guarded by phalanxes of armed

109

men. Candidates for election must fear to mingle with the crowds. Clearly, violence is intrusive, pervasive, powerful and pernicious.

Today's Torah Reading provides a point of departure to address the problem of violence and its ramifications.

The Reading today speaks of the twin brothers, Jacob and Esau. Jacob, ancestor of the Jewish people, is characterized as a gentle and home-oriented person, whereas his twin Esau is described as violent, *"an expert hunter, an outdoor man"* (Gen. 25:27). The ancient sages go beyond the plain meaning of the text to stress the violence in Esau's nature. Esau is a shedder of blood, ruthless, a cruel warrior, the progenitor of Rome. Rebecca, the mother of both, is determined that Jacob shall receive his father's blessing, and thus become the official heir of Abraham and his successor in the covenant with God. Isaac, however, blind with old age, prefers Esau. Rebecca therefore, resorts to deception: Jacob is to impersonate Esau. Since Isaac may rely on his sense of touch to identify the intended recipient of his blessing, Jacob is dressed in Esau's clothes and his smooth arms and neck are covered with kid hide, undistinguishable from the hairy skin of his rough twin. The trick is successful: Jacob receives the blessing. When later on the unsuspecting Esau arrives to claim the blessing from his father, Isaac realizes he has been fooled. He is shattered. *"Isaac was seized by an exceedingly violent trembling"* (Gen. 27:33).

The ancient Rabbis make a strange comment on the text (Midrash Tanchuma Toldot 13). Twice in his life, they say, Isaac trembled: the first time when he lay bound on the altar before his father Abraham, about to be sacrificed in obedience to God's command, saved only at the very last moment through God's intervention. The second time he trembled was when Isaac discovered he had been tricked. *"When did he tremble more?"* the Sages ask. They answer that on this occasion he must have trembled more, it being described as *"an exceedingly violent trembling."*

Why did Isaac react so strongly to his discovery of the deception? The Rashbam, a classical commentator, who always aims at the primary meaning of the text, explains: *"because he had found hairy skin on Jacob's neck."* He trembled, shocked and frightened because of the erroneous perception that Jacob, the gentle one, had become like his brother Esau: a hairy savage, a violent huntsman. Facing death on the altar of sacrifice, Isaac had not trembled as much as he did when he thought that in competition with Esau, Jacob had adopted the violent character of his twin!

110

Our Sages believed that history was a struggle of Rome against Jerusalem. The competition between Jacob and Esau had been the antecedent of this struggle; the messianic era would bring its resolution. Rome was the city of blood, capital of an empire based on the expendability of human lives, on cruelty, slavery and savagery. Jerusalem was the antithesis of Rome. It was the City of Peace, the home of the spirit. It was the city where the sanctity of human life had blossomed, on whose streets the prophets had proclaimed *"Not by might and not by power, but by my spirit, says the Lord"* (Zech. 4:6), and*"They shall forge their swords into ploughshares...nation shall not raise a sword against nation, neither shall they learn war any more"* (Micah 4:3).

Israel today is a besieged society. Under the constant threat of terrorism it is surrounded by enemies pledged to its destruction. It does not behoove us, safe on the sidelines in Canada, to give Israelis advice on how to meet the peril and how to defend themselves. A country, where a package abandoned on a bus is not a case for the lost-and-found office but for a hasty evacuation of the bus, may question our competence to give advice on security measures.

All the same, I must sound one warning: the real danger to survival- the greater cause for trembling- is the possibility that Jews might become like their enemies; that Jews might turn into their opposites. Whenever Jerusalem imitates Rome, when Jacob impersonates Esau, we are in extreme peril.

I am not a pacifist. I believe that the defence of its citizens is the first duty of every state. I believe that Israel must maintain its military strength. I am proud of Israel's victories and of the bravery, boldness and skill of its defenders. Yet, I also believe that Israel's enemies on the outside are less dangerous than the enemy from within: the loss of idealism, the erosion of the Zionist ethos, the decline of Jewish spirituality. If Rome could turn Jerusalem into another Rome, that would be Rome's absolute victory and our ultimate defeat.

My heart trembles when I read that Israel has become a first-rank arms supplier of the Third World. Naturally, I know that export is a prime economic necessity for Israel and that it cannot afford to be squeamish; naturally, I am happy that Israel's industrial technology has achieved success – but my heart trembles if to survive we have to supply the tools of Esau's trade. My heart trembles when Jewish terrorists kill innocent people and when Jewish terrorism is defended by so-called religious elements. My heart trembles when a rabbi, member of the Knesset, and his followers espouse and practice the policy of terrorizing Israeli Arabs into leaving their homes in a land of which they too are citizens. They are inflicting on others what we suffered through history; they are emulating our oppressors in a tragic reversal of roles.

If Jacob must become Esau to survive, survival itself may no longer be worthwhile.

My Jewish faith informs me to the contrary: only as Jacob can we survive. The Esaus of the world have all perished; only Jacob received God's assurance of eternal survival:

> But you,
> Have no fear, My servant Jacob
> -declares the Lord-
> ... For I am with you to deliver you ...
> I will make an end of all the nations
> Among which I have dispersed you;
> But I will not make an end of you,
> Though I will discipline you in justice
> Not leaving you immune from punishment.
> *(Jeremiah 30:10-11)*

Have no fear, My servant Jacob!

---

[1] *The reference is to Indira Ghandi. The assassiniation of her son and successor was still in the future.*

Stop and Live!

"I am too busy."

Sometimes, it's an alibi to avoid an unpleasant task.

Sometimes, it is the bitter truth.

Many people are too busy, always on the move. Serious about their work and conscientious about their performance, they deprive themselves of contemplative interludes. Their days become endless rounds of one task after another. They run on a treadmill that refuses to stop.

In sermons on the topic of being too busy, I have often pointed to the rhythm imposed by the Jewish calendar as a remedy. Shabbat is the weekly contemplative renewal. The festivals provide additional opportunities of breaking the vicious cycle of our frantic life style.

I once read a brief Chasidic tract offering rules for daily living which I put aside for future reference. The time to adapt it for a sermon came when I pondered the meaning of the Festival called Shmini Atzeret, a peculiarly nondescript holy day identified simply as the "Eighth Day of the Feast" - an afterthought, as it were, to the Sukkot Festival. Suddenly, I caught a different nuance of the word "Atzeret." It had reminded me of stop signs in Israel.

Being too busy has always been one of my many faults. Sermons addressed to oneself are often most effective in reaching the hearts and minds of others. So it was with this sermon which had grown out of my own distress.

Stop and Live! ────────────────
A Sermon preached on Shmini Atzeret 5747 - 1986

"Atzor" is the word stencilled on stop signs at Israeli intersections.

Though you would not always know it from the behaviour of Israeli motorists, "Atzor" means "Stop!"

The word comes from the same root as the second word in the name of the festival "Shmini Atzeret - The Eighth Day of 'Assembly.'" In the Hebrew of the Bible, the root of the word means "to restrain,

113

to hold back, to close up." Though the precise meaning is unclear, "Atzeret" is therefore usually rendered as "Assembly."

The modern utilization of the word in stop signs is quite relevant to the significance of the Festival as it emerges from the classical commentaries.

Shmini Atzeret occurs at the end of an exciting season of Holy Days. Our emotions have been exercised. We have experienced the anticipatory anxiety of Rosh Hashana and the seriousness of Yom Kippur. For the seven days of Sukkot we have been high on the crest of joy. Now, it's finished. We're ready to go home!

Says God: "Stop! One moment please. Before you go, stop once more and stay for one more day" (Rashi Leviticus 23:36).

Alas, an extra day – even with the addition of Simchat Torah- cannot delay our re-entry into the normal world indefinitely. Sooner or later, we must return from our festive orbit to the world of normal routine. The usual problems, aggravations and nuisances will promptly reclaim our attention and strain our energies.

What use is the extra day?

Let me suggest therefore that the purpose of Shmini Atzeret is not just the brief respite of a one-day stop. Rather, the extra day is a hint that we ought to program a daily Atzeret - a creative, restorative stop - into our normal routine.

Like the stop sign at an intersection, a daily Atzeret could reduce our excessive speed and save us from collisions and break-downs.

The other day, I came across a Chasidic check list of questions we ought to ask ourselves every day as an aid for spiritual perfection. It occurred to me that with some minor modifications these questions could serve as a formula for coping with stress and achieving a healthy mental and emotional balance.

In adapting this Chasidic guide for this purpose and in keeping with the festival of Shmini Atzeret, I expanded the number of questions to eight. I have eight questions for you. If you can answer them affirmatively every day, or at least most days, you will be more fully equipped to get through your days and nights. You will be better able to cope with your problems and to protect your emotional and physical health.

114

** **DID YOU PRAY TODAY?** Your day gets off to a special start if it begins with prayer, enhanced by donning Tallit and Tefillin if applicable. If you can join a "minyan," it is especially effective, but even if you pray in the privacy of your home, prayer is beneficial. At any time during the day, you may take a few minutes to reflect, to articulate and review your needs and mention them to God.

** **DID YOU STUDY TORAH TODAY?** A period of study, brief or prolonged, works wonders. Your mind is diverted from the utilitarian and the trivial. You turn instead to the eternal. Read a chapter from the Bible! Ponder a thought-provoking story from the Midrash. Open one of the hundreds of Jewish books available in English or in Hebrew if you can handle it. Make it part of your routine.

** **DID YOU GIVE TZEDAKA TODAY?** I don't mean the once-in-a-while big cheque. No day should pass without your giving to a good cause or needy person. If you cannot give every day directly, keep a charity box in which to deposit a daily gift for periodic distribution, but perform the act of giving every day. It is better to give one dollar a day than seven dollars a week. It is the daily giving that contributes to your own serenity.

** **DID YOU HAVE A MOMENT OF SOLITUDE TODAY?** Chasidim call it *"Hitbodedut"* - a withdrawal from human companionship into a state of being alone with yourself. Find solitude in a park, on a walk through a quiet street and talk to yourself. Think. Reflect. Dream. What a healing force flows from solitude! You are released from the pressure of another presence. Your own inner self is restored as you relax alone in your private world.

** **DID YOU SPEND SOME TIME HELPING ANOTHER PERSON?** Take the time to visit a sick friend or a stranger who is in hospital and in need of company. Have you phoned someone today who hungers for a word of encouragement? Have you made someone feel better by making a cheerful remark or a complimentary comment? It is not hard. Perhaps you can go shopping for someone for whom shopping is difficult, or you might offer to go with someone who would enjoy your company or expertise.

** **DID YOU SEEK AN EMOTIONAL EXPERIENCE TODAY?** Every day you ought to provide some nourishment for your emotions, for that part of you that responds to art and to sensual

115

enjoyment. Emotional experiences are important in your life. Listen to a piece of music that stimulates your feelings. Sing one of your favourite songs. Read or recite a poem. Take the time to look at a good piece of art and let it speak to you. Devote some of your leisure time to reading a good book.

** DID YOU ENGAGE IN A HEALTHFUL PHYSICAL ACTIVITY? The ravages of stressful living can often be reversed or prevented by the healing exertion through physical activity. Take off time for a walk, a run, a swim, a game of tennis, a round of golf. The human body is God's creation; it deserves care and respect. Make exercise part of your life style. It will improve not only your physical condition, but will heighten mental freshness, enthusiasm and joy. Physical fitness enhances your creativity and adds zest to your life.

** DID YOU REMEMBER A DEPARTED? Remembrance of the dead is not only appropriate at Yizkor time and other rare occasions. Just as we think of friends whose company and conversation we can enjoy, we must also think of those who are gone from our presence. Make a deliberate effort every day to focus for a few moments on the memory of a deceased person. Think of a parent, or a grandparent who is no longer, a relative or a friend whom you lost. Concentrate on one person at a time; allow yourself to feel the aura of that person; let the memory envelop you. You may feel a calming effect; a breath of peace may brush over you. Remembering may help you gain a better perspective on your own life.

Asking yourself daily these eight questions and changing your life so that you may answer them affirmatively will not solve all your serious problems. But it will become a habit that helps you cope with the strain and stress of life situations. It will help you brush aside the little irritations and soothe the abrasions which otherwise may add up and threaten to overwhelm you.

To rise above the daily nuisances, to achieve equanimity in the confusing turmoil surrounding us, observe a daily "Atzeret": Stop, and ask yourself eight questions!

116

Justice More or Less

The sermon "Justice More or Less" originated while I was studying the first chapter of the Talmudic tractate "Sanhedrin" with a group of people. A passage suggested to me that Justice might be situational, or relative.

Suddenly, I had a mental flash-back: I recalled a fragment of an essay on Justice and Society I wrote as a teenager.

The sermon "Justice More or Less" was the result.

Justice More or Less ―――――――――
Preached on Parshat Shoftim 5751 - 1991

> *Justice, justice only , you must pursue so that you may live and inherit the land which the Lord your God is about to give you.*
>
> *(Deuteronomy 16:20)*

When we were young, idealistic and prone to indulge in meta-physical speculation and passionate debates over abstract propo-sitions and philosophical issues, we would often debate the con-cept of Justice. Is justice an absolute ideal, the supreme principle to which everything else is subordinate, or is justice meant to serve society, and therefore might it be modified or compromised when the social welfare demands it? Must justice be done regardless of consequences, even if it harms the community or is detrimental to the well-being of vulnerable individuals whom we would like to protect? Or is the community, and particularly the State, above justice? Does the interest of the State define what justice is?

Growing up in the nineteen-thirties against the background of totalitarianism, we pursued this debate with more than theoretical interest. We had read and studied many of the pertinent German philosophers and authors, poets and playwrights. In the High

School classes of the Third Reich, this debate was gradually quenched by the Nazi doctrines which preached the superiority of the State and absolute loyalty to the Führer whose will transcended bourgeois justice. But in the arena of the Jewish Youth Movement we could still joust with the weapons of the classical philosophers and the teachers of humanist enlightenment. We could still listen to the thrust-and-parry of verbal swords and shields in the contests between the Marxism of Hashomer Hatzair and the last defenders of German Romantic Idealism.

"Fiat justitia et pereat mundus! - Let Justice be done though the world perish!" is the Latin dictum preserved in my memory that summed up my youthfully idealistic position.

Now we are older and more pragmatic. We no longer have the spirit to cling to absolute idealistic positions that appear to be out of touch with reality. Yes, justice must be blind, impartial and unconditional. It must remain one of the high, overriding principles that order life and society.

Yet ought it not be tempered sometimes with mercy, common sense or practical considerations? Is it really still justice, if it becomes counterproductive, thereby undermining the peace and welfare of the community?

Is it wrong for the president of Argentina to grant a pardon to the generals responsible for the murder of thousands of victims of the "dirty war" if it is the only way of preserving democracy in the country against a take-over by the Army?

Should we prosecute a poor single mother of four children because she was caught shoplifting a silk blouse she could never afford to buy?

According to the Torah, there is one law for all: neither the rich nor the poor must receive favouritism in judgement. And yet, would it be justice to throw the full weight of the law at the wretched person who in her distress and misery lost out to temptation?

In the course of time, I learned that similar debates must have been carried on by the Jewish sages of antiquity. *"Yikkov haddin et hahar! - Let the Law -or Justice- pierce the mountain!"* the Talmud proposes (Sanhedrin 6 b). Justice must take its course regardless of consequences. Law does not compromise. The ideal must shape the real, not the other way around.

118

Halacha -Jewish Law- finds a detour around the mountain when circumstances warrant it, despite its unrelenting commitment to equal justice and to its priority over other values. For example, the laws of Kashrut recognize what some scholars call "extra-halachic" considerations, i.e. considerations standing outside the perimeters of Halacha, in order to alleviate hardships that would result from an impartial application of the rules. I prefer not to call these considerations "extra-halachic," but rather built-in modifiers which attenuate the impartially blind application of the rules when compassionate reasons exist. In order to avert economic hardship and ruinous loss to an individual, Kashrut provisions may be applied leniently, even when such leniency rests on shaky Halachic ground. "Bend the Law and let the world not perish!" might be the dictum implicit in such cases.

The principle that the welfare of society may permit deviation from the rules of justice is illustrated clearly at the very beginning of the Talmud Tractate Sanhedrin, which deals with the administration of justice.

It is taught (Sanhedrin 2b), that the rules of justice demand that witnesses be examined with the same rigorous thoroughness in money disputes as in cases of capital crimes. Truth is truth, and therefore it must be ascertained for the sake of justice, irrespective of the substance of a law case, whether the life of the accused, or the property of a litigant is at stake. However, Rabbi Hanina, an important Talmudic teacher waives this rule in the case of disputed loans, so as *"not to shut the door in the faces of would-be borrowers."* If we insisted on subjecting witnesses in the case of a defaulted loan to the same scrutiny as in capital cases and thus made it difficult to win a judgement against a defaulting debtor, people would become reluctant to grant loans to individuals who need them. This would be a disservice to the poor, who are the potential borrowers. The overall aim of the Torah to create a compassionate society would thus be subverted. Rabbi Hanina advises us to sacrifice a degree of justice to the welfare of society!

Similarly, the Talmud proposes that the criteria for the selection of judges be lowered in the case of disputes involving loans so as not to make the judicial process unduly cumbersome and thus pervert the objective of making loans more easily available.

Is Justice then situational? Is it merely relative? Does the answer to the question "What is justice?" start with "It depends ..."?

Not at all. Justice is absolute. It is neither the tool of the state nor the servant of society. Its principles cannot be compromised because of convenience or "higher" needs, for there is nothing higher. But the implementation of justice, its application to human affairs- and especially to the "lower" stratum of society- must not lead to absurdity, callousness and cruelty. Our Sages taught that God himself had to limit his own Absoluteness so that the world could exist, and had to curb justice in order to make it possible for human life to unfold. Reasonableness, compassion and realistic regard for its ultimate goals will establish justice without destroying the world.

The Agenda of Silence

Most congregational rabbis face a dilemma before the High Holidays: the selection of sermon topics.

This is the time when the Rabbi speaks to the largest proportion of his membership. The Synagogue is full. It is natural, therefore, that he would like to reserve the messages he deems most important for these occasions.

The temptation is strong, therefore, to concentrate on topics of global dimensions, on the issues which concern the future, the survival of humanity and civilization. The threat of nuclear extinction, the problems of the environment, world peace, human rights, freedom, political and social issues of universal concern, rank high in the rabbinic hierarchy of urgency. Moreover, the Rabbi feels responsible for making it clear and for reminding his congregation that religion in the twentieth century is profoundly concerned with these issues. Too many congregants persist in the old-fashioned belief that religion engages mainly in spiritual, other-worldly matters; that religion is and ought to be ecclesiastical, concentrating on ritual, rites of passage and abstract theological beliefs.

On the other hand, the global issues, important to religion though they are, fill the columns and pages of the newspapers and magazines the congregants read. Thus, Rabbinic treatment of the same issues courts redundancy. More importantly, these are the issues which the individual is least able to control or affect. What can the average man and woman in the congregation, burdened with the task of making a living and raising a family, do about world peace and nuclear proliferation? Are the High Holidays not the occasion to speak to the personal issues, to the problems of the individual, and to his faith in God in his every-day life?

Rabbinic communications I had received in the mail during 1987 gave me the impression that the global issues had won the competition for the attention of my colleagues on the "Days of Awe." I recoiled from the one-sided emphasis. I decided to stress themes that would be more relevant to individual decision-making on the threshold of the New Year.

The year 1987 was also the time when "White Collar Crime" ranked high in public awareness. There was a series of scandals involving stock market manipulations. Dishonesty on the part of individuals in position of trust in the board rooms of the nation were common. All these sensational exposures of fraudulent practices in commerce and in the securities exchanges laid bare an abominable indifference to ethics in the business and professional communities. Jewish people were by no means exempt from this type of criminality. Greed, and the abuses encouraged by it, seemed to threaten the integrity not only of the financial elite, but also of the ordinary person trying to make a living.

It was time to remind congregants of some Jewish basics. My sermon entitled "The Agenda of Silence" was the result.

The Agenda of Silence

Preached on Rosh Hashana 5748 - 1987

ובשופר גדול יתקע וקול דממה דקה ישמע

Uv-shofar gadol yitaka, v-kol demama dakka yishama -
A great Shofar is sounded, and the sound of a hushed silence is heard!

(from the Mahzor)

Rosh Hashana presents a paradox.

With one ear, we hear the *"Great Shofar,"* the signal of Redemption. It announces a public and universal agenda: the Kingdom of God, the New World Order.

With the other ear, we hear the *"Kol demama dakka - the sound of hushed silence,"* whispering a different agenda to be transacted in the stillness of the heart.

The phrase *"Kol demama dakka"* comes from the story of the prophet Elijah (IKings 19:9ff).

The prophet is in the depth of a personal crisis. His mission has failed. He is a hunted man, discouraged and burnt out.

At that crucial moment, God grants him a theophany: an encounter with God's presence, a glimpse of the divine nature. The prophet is transformed by this experience. His questions and his doubts become irrelevant. His broken spirit is healed; his courage and zeal are restored.

How did God's presence manifest itself to Elijah?

> *A strong and mighty wind was levelling mountains and shattering rocks; but God was not in the wind. After the wind, there came an earthquake, but God was not in the earthquake. After the earthquake there came a fire, but God was not in the fire, and after the fire, there followed the sound of a hushed silence. As soon as Elijah heard it, he wrapped his face in his mantle, stepped forward and stood by the mouth of the cave.*

What a pity that we are unable to hear the "Kol Demama Dakka, the sound of hushed silence! Our ears are tuned to the "Shofar Gadol," to the "Great Shofar" of the mass media trumpeting the big issues, the storm, the earthquake and the fire. Our pulpits, alas, echo the themes.

Yet our deepest need on Rosh Hashana is similar to Elijah's. We need a revival of faith, a renewal of spiritual energy. We must address the agenda of silence. This is the time for "Cheshbon Hanefesh," the inspired Hebrew expression for taking an "Inventory of the Soul."

Our priority today is not the clean-up of our physical environment, but the pollution control of the heart. At other times, we may worry about the survival of our lakes; today we are called to neutralize the acid rain that corrodes our soul.

Today our main worry as Jews is neither our physical survival nor our capability to generate headlines and to exercise political power.

Our greatest need is the revival of true Jewish personal piety.

It is our moral viability that hangs in balance today; at stake is our survival as a people whose life force is morality.

Let me put it bluntly: I am afraid that Jews in general are becoming selfish, materialistic and opportunistic.

I am afraid that for many Jews, hedonism has effectively replaced the spiritual, altruistic and ethical values of Judaism. Expediency substitutes for principle.

What does it really mean to be a Jew?

The Book of Job tells us of a prosperous individual, by the name of Job, who in quick succession loses all his possessions, then his children, and then is stricken by a noxious, itchy skin disease.

His friends come to comfort him and to talk. "God is just," they say, "so your condition must be due to sin. Everybody sins. Just repent and confess; God will forgive you, heal you and restore your good fortune!"

But Job refuses to compromise his integrity. He will not lie, even to please God. Truthfulness does not permit him to confess sins he has not committed. His friends' insinuations compel him to list his deeds of righteousness. The result is a veritable catalogue of morality which has made the twenty-ninth chapter of the Book of Job one of the most often-quoted passages of the Bible:

> *I saved the poor man who cried out,*
> *the orphan who had none to help him.*
> *I received the blessing of the lost;*
> *I gladdened the heart of the widow.*
> *I clothed myself in righteousness and it robed me;*
> *justice was my cloak and my turban.*
> *I was eyes to the blind,*
> *and feet to the lame,*
> *I was a father to the needy,*
> *and I looked into the case of the stranger.*
> *I broke the jaw of the wrongdoer,*
> *and I wrested prey from his teeth.* (Job 29:12-17)

Is it not remarkable that Job defines personal piety purely in terms of scrupulous ethical behaviour? His catalogue of righteousness contains no reference to prayer, to sacrifice or other ritual observance. Kindness and compassion are the essentials of piety.

The Rabbinic view does not differ materially from the Biblical. According to the Talmudic Sages, the first question asked of the human being who appears before the Divine Judge is *"Did you conduct your business dealings in good faith?"* God's first test does not relate to the candidate's observance of the dietary laws, nor to any part of his ritual conduct, but his honesty in business!

On a Yom Kippur, in a small town – so the story goes – two Jews left their synagogue for a breath of fresh air. They saw two other

Jews coming out of the neighbouring Reform temple and heading for a restaurant. An argument ensued:

"How can you eat on Yom Kippur?"

"We are Reform Jews. Judaism is ethical monotheism, our Rabbi tells us. That means we believe in one God whom we worship not by rituals, but by ethical conduct. We carry on our business with honesty all year. So we need not bother fasting!"

The Reform Jews enter the restaurant, while the other two continue their walk. Said one to the other: "What fools these Reform Jews are! For the sake of one silly meal, they practice honesty all year long!"

This story encapsulates two unfortunate fallacies.

The first is the assumption that moral rectitude obviates compliance with ritual Mitzvot. Jews do not have an exclusive claim on morality. While personal ethics are an absolute requirement of Judaism, adherence to ethics alone does not make you Jewish. Observance of Shabbat, of Kashrut, of circumcision, of Jewish prayer are the identifying signs of Jewishness. Several Mitzvot are therefore designated in the Torah as "*Ot,*" as "signs."

The Shabbat is a "sign"; Tefillin are called a "sign," incidentally the reason why Tefillin are redundant and therefore not worn on Shabbat.

Circumcision is the "sign" of the covenant.

Rituals are our marks of identity. Mitzvot, the sacred acts, help to create the distinctiveness without which we cannot survive.

Different is the fallacy of the two observant Jews in the story. They fail to realize that fasting on Yom Kippur, as well as the observance of the other ritual laws, is nearly meaningless if it is not joined with the observance of the commandments that govern interpersonal relationships, the *"Mitzvot bein adam lachavero - between one human being and his fellow."*

God forgives ritual sins readily. However, sins that bring harm to others, that inflict insult or hurt on our fellow human beings, require as a precondition for divine pardon the making of apologies and amends, as well as forgiveness by the victims.

The flourishing of a black market in Jerusalem may be a worse sin in God's sight than open cinemas on Shabbat.

125

The Kashrut of the dollar we earn is no less important than Kashrut of the steak we eat.

Rabbi Aryeh Levin was a famous Jerusalem Rabbi till his death in 1969. His biography, by Simcha Raz, is entitled *"A Tzaddik in Our Time."* As the author notes, what made Rabbi Levin a Tzaddik was not his meticulous observance of Mitzvot. Of course, he observed the laws meticulously, as do thousands of others without being called "Tzaddik." He was called a Tzaddik because he looked after prisoners in jail and after their families; because he cared for the bereaved, the lonely, the poor, not by handing out money -he had but little- but with his presence and personal acts of kindness.

One miserable December night, his biographer relates, during a specially cold and wet winter, a cantor by the name of Weinberger met him on a cemetery, walking in a funeral procession. It was on a Saturday night, when funerals are frequently held in Jerusalem because it is not customary to leave a corpse overnight in Jerusalem. "Reb Aryeh, what are you doing here on such a miserable winter night?" exclaimed Cantor Weinberger, "The deceased must be a close relative of yours!"

"Oh no," replied Rabbi Levin, "he is no relation whatsoever. In fact, I don't even know whose funeral this is. But close to my home, in my poor neighbourhood, I heard someone trying to round up people for a funeral: 'Gute Yiden, kummt tzu ein levayah! Kumt tzu bagleiten a mes! (Good Jews, come to a funeral! Come to escort the dead!) So I understood that they were short of a 'minyan' for a funeral and I thought to myself: Who will come out on such a miserable night to the funeral of an unknown man? There will not even be a 'minyan!' So I came."

In his Introduction the author writes, "Of material property and wealth, he had nothing of his own to speak of. Yet he was among the richest of men. He gave more than the greatest philanthropist and donor of charity. He gave of himself. He dispensed love and esteem generously to all."

All of us can be religious Jews. Everyone can listen for the "Kol Demama Dakka - the hushed voice of silence." We can bare our heart to the still encounter.

We can address the quiet agenda.

We can choose to live in integrity and with compassion.

126

Be kind to others! Be faithful to parents when they age!

You can be a Tzaddik! When your friend is in trouble, do not shun him, but go and talk to him.

There are so many shut-ins. So many men and women are prisoners behind the walls of loneliness. Sick people often suffer more from abandonment than from their illness.

An overworked young mother might need your helping hand.

Take an older person for a walk, or treat him to a ball game.

If you are retired, you might remember a friend who could use your help in his store for a day.

There is so much we can do. No Great Shofars will sound. No global problem will be solved. The acid rain will remain.

But our world will be a better one, more worthy to survive, and a heartbeat closer to the Kingdom of the Lord.

Does God Know You?

In our Synagogue, the attendance on the eighth day of Pesach rivals that of the High Holy Days. Extra seating has to be provided. By the time the sermon is delivered, just before the Yizkor Prayers, the sanctuary is filled to overflowing.

1989 was my last year as Senior Rabbi of Adath Israel. My successor having been chosen, I was to assume the honourary position of Rabbi Emeritus on September the first, forty-two years to the day after I had begun my Rabbinic career with the same congregation.

When I prepared my sermon for the eighth day of Passover, I was aware of the fact that this would be my last opportunity to address such a large congregation as the Senior Rabbi. Although I would have many future opportunities to preach as Rabbi Emeritus, I felt the need of "summing up." Of course, I did not attempt to compress in one sermon the essence of my teaching over the years, but I wanted to leave the congregation with a significant message that might epitomize many of the ideas and values I had tried to communicate during the course of my time.

I was very pleased with the result. My sermon "Does God Know You?" represents my thinking on a number of important issues. It touches serious theological topics relevant to the experience of many people. How do we face undeserved evil? What is God's role in it? What is the importance of Mitzvot in our relationship to God?

In addition, it was a sermon that used classical texts extensively to carry forward the thought. I was able to interpret these texts with some originality in dealing with an unusual concept: what it means to be known by God.

It is one of my favourite sermons.

Does God Know You? _____
A Sermon preached at Yizkor Services on Passover 1989

I wanted to tease my friend Seemour [1] a little when he asked me about the topic of my sermon.

"I am going to talk about a Lamborghini," I said.

"What in heaven is a Lamberghini?"

I feigned surprise.

"You, supposedly a man of the world, do not know what a Lamborghini is! It's a famous automobile! I saw one parked last week in front of the Synagogue. The kids at the Kiddush were all excited, and insisted that I go out to look at the marvel. It was indeed a sleek, beautiful, powerful-looking white machine; really a dream car. It was also parked on the "No Parking" side of the street, but I guess when you drive a Lamborghini, you don't worry about a ticket. The kids told me it costs more than a hundred thousand dollars."

To keep Seemour curious, I did not tell him any more about the sermon. But in my mind, the dream car had set in motion a train of thought that started from a passage of the Torah portion we had read that day and connected with Pesach.

At first glance, it appears to be a primitive notion: the Israelites had to smear the blood of the Passover lamb on the lintel and the door posts of their houses in Egypt. *"When I see the blood,"* God assures them, *"I will pass over you"* (Exodus 12:13). He will see the sign of the blood on the door and will "pass over" without killing the first-born, whom he will smite in the homes of the Egyptians. The name "Pesach," Passover in English, is derived from this passage.

The question is obvious. Does God need a visible sign on the door to distinguish between the house of an Israelite and an Egyptian house?

Rashi, quoting a Midrash, offers an answer: *"'When I look at you,'* God says, *'I want to see you engaged in the performance of my commandments.'"* In other words, God gives them a commandment, a Mitzva, to fulfil so as to provide Him with a reason to spare the Israelite homes during his nocturnal passage through the streets of Egypt. The answer is to the point, but not quite satisfactory.

The Mechilta (on Exodus 12:7,13), one of the ancient Midrashic commentaries, presents a different interpretation. The text says: *"V'haya hadam lachem l'ot - the blood shall be a sign for you."* Here, the Mechilta picks up a nuance: *"LACHEM l'ot, v'lo la-acheirim l'ot - it shall be a sign FOR YOU, not for others - from this we infer that the blood was to be applied 'mi-bifnim' - on the INSIDE of the lintel"* - not on the outside, visible to others. It was a sign for the people *inside* the house -*"lachem - for you,"* not for anyone outside, and certainly not for God who does not require an outward sign.

Allow me to share a painful experience with you. I am called upon to comfort a family in shock. A young person has just been killed in a traffic accident. The distraught mother whispers to me through her sobs: "God was not looking!"

The accident was a lapse of divine attention. It was a mishap in God's providence. It was not the driver who failed to look, who took a foolish chance, but it was God who had an accident.

To my thinking, the notion that God may have lost control makes a tragedy unbearable. Some modern theologians attempt to relieve God of responsibility for evil in this manner. He is not "almighty," they say, not in complete control. I doubt that this idea alleviates the pain, nor is it theologically sound. You cannot defend God by denying his final control. If he relinquished control, why did he? If he never had control, he is not God. It is less difficult to cope with tragedy if we can believe that God was indeed looking, that misadventure is not due to blind chance but is a part of a providential pattern, albeit beyond our discernment.

A few weeks ago, the Shabbat Torah reading recorded the tragedy of Aaron's sons, who suffered mysterious sudden death while they officiated for the first time as priests in the Sanctuary.

Moses tried to comfort his brother Aaron. *"'God is hallowed by his closest servants,'"* he said (Leviticus 10:3), *"and Aaron was silent."*

What did Moses say that enabled him to assuage his brother's grief? What was the magic word that stilled Aaron's complaint?

Our Sages offer a deeply meaningful explanation. Moses was able to convey to his brother that the tragedy was not a random accident.

> *When Aaron understood that his children were "yedu'ei makom- known to God," he kept silent*
> (Talmud Zevachim 115b).

130

This is indeed an extraordinary thought and a very comforting one.

There are people who are *"yedu'ei makom - known to God."* Nothing bad can "happen" to them. For them, there are no "accidents," for God is aware of them. Whatever befell them, it is impossible that God was not looking!

By implication, there are then also people who are unknown to God! If we were to pray for one of them, our prayer might be returned unopened with the notation "Unknown!" We have never heard of him!

There are people who have never come to God's attention.

Clearly, we must live so that God comes to know us. We must come to His notice. We must strive to become *"yedu'ei makom."*

How do we come to God's notice?

Things that catch human eyes do not catch God's attention.

> *He does not prize the strength of horses,*
> *nor does He value the fleetness of men;*
> *but the Lord values those who fear Him,*
> *those who depend on His faithful care.*
> *(Psalms 147:10)*

Clearly, driving a Lamborghini does not introduce us to God.

What we do to impress others, does not impress God. Conspicuous ostentation does not make us conspicuous to God.

"Lachem l'ot, v'lo la-acheirim l'ot - the sign is for you, not for others." The significant mark for God is not a billboard advertisement to the world, *"ela mi-bifnim - but on the inside."* Signs on the outside do not make us known to God, only the signs within.

The Israelites in Egypt, in order to become worthy of the Exodus, had to make themselves known to God. It was not God who needed the sign of blood daubed on the door; the Israelites needed the Mitzva, never having done one before; and this Mitzva they had to perform inside their home, *"mi-bifnim - within,"* without publicity, in order to become known to God.

Mitzvot make us known to God, especially those we do *"mi-bifnim"*: inwardly, discreetly, privately and modestly.

131

People who give of themselves become known to God. God knows the person who works hard to support his family, who lives with decency and honesty, and does his share for others, but makes no headlines, attracts no publicity. Few of his contemporaries may hear of him, but God knows him.

My friends, make yourselves known to God! I appeal to you: do Mitzvot! Practice "Tzedaka," righteousness through deeds of loving kindness and social responsibility! And do it without ostentation!

Before Pesach, a congregant gave me $3,000 with the instruction to distribute the money to poor people in need of food for Passover, of course without mentioning the donor. Such a person will be known to God! However, it is not the magnitude of the gift that impresses God, *"ela mi-bifnim - but that which is within."*

Attend Synagogue regularly. Prayer uttered sincerely, with humility, is one good way of coming to God's attention. How wonderful it is to see you all in our Synagogue today, on the last day of Pessach when we recite the Yizkor Memorial Prayers! Coming often, regularly, not only on the high points of the religious year, will make you known to God.

In a few months, I will hand over the spiritual trusteeship of our congregation to my successor. How good will I feel, if at that time I could entrust him with a true Adath Israel: a community of men, women and children, all known to God and secure in the certainty of His providence and love!

---

1 *My friend Seemour materializes conveniently when I need a foil for the development of my thought, or when I would welcome a question as an excuse for a sharp turn. Seemour is useful when I want to explain a point before I really start, so as to avoid disturbing the flow of ideas later on. Sometimes, his visits enable me to present a rationale for the choice of my topic, since Seemour is not too bashful to make suggestions which may reflect the interest of my listeners. My conversations with Seemour may take my listeners right into my sermon workshop and let them share in the formation of my ideas. Seemour -his name is also spelled Seymore, but never Seymour- is a very good friend: always there when I need him, and only then!*

The Terrible 2's

Experience has taught me over the years to ease up on the demands my sermons make on the intellectual and cognitive capacity of the congregation when the time comes around for the last sermon of Yom Kippur.

Ponderous themes may have been discussed on Rosh Hashana and at the Kol Nidre and Morning Services of Yom Kippur. However, when we reach the late afternoon, the large crowd of worshippers that has gathered for the final phase of the day's enterprise is tired in body, worn out from the long fast, yet waiting for an emotional climax. My practice has been to offer then a sermon that is easy to follow, down to earth, with its ideas lying well within the congregants' own experience. I try to discuss issues with which my listeners can easily identify.

Sometimes I draw on a story or on a personal experience to make my point. In any event, I try to evoke feelings and create empathy. A touch of humour or whimsy often serves the purpose well.

"The Terrible 2's" filled my requirements. It was simple in structure and thought; the congregation could easily identify with the ideas presented. Moreover, the sermon had personal relevance to no one more than myself!

The pun in its title made it easy to remember.

The Terrible 2's
A Sermon Preached before Ne'ilah on Yom Kippur
1987 - 5748

At the age of two, children discover their autonomy, the capacity to exercise their own independent will. Parents call this stage "the Terrible Two's," as they wait resignedly for the two-year-old to turn three.

The Terrible Two's I have in mind are not so easily put behind us.

One of the most solemn prayers that the Chazan recites on the High Holy Days is popularly known by its first word: *"Hin'ni - Here I am!"* It is a word made famous by Abraham, our patriarch, who

133

responded to God's call with the same word: "Here I am! At your service; unreservedly, unconditionally!" (Genesis 22:1).

"Here I am, poor in deeds, trembling and afraid," the Chazan sings, but despite his fear and sense of unworthiness, he is ready to undertake his mission.

Nowadays, *"Hin'ni"* is not a popular word. The very opposite phrase is the more likely response when a person is summoned to undertake voluntarily a challenging and idealistic task.

It is the phrase "Not me!"

Not me! On me you should not count!

If we press for a rationalization of the refusal, we will probably hear an excuse that pivots on the word "too."

"Come to Shabbat services!" I tried to entice a congregant recently.

"Sorry, Rabbi!" was the reply. "I am too impatient! I cannot sit through a service."

No doubt, many people really are impatient. They have been conditioned by the pace of modern life.

We want things instantaneously. We cannot wait. We expect instant gratification.

Some people are too impatient to listen to "Boobie,"–grandmother by any other name– tell her stories. What treasures of memory and personal history they may miss! Children are too impatient to attend their Jewish school. Young people are too impatient to defer the chance of "making real money" and refuse to accept the academic discipline required by three or four years in college or university.

"Too young" is another Terrible Too.

Called to be God's prophet, the reluctant Jeremiah tried to take refuge behind his youth. "I am but a youth," Jeremiah pleaded (Jeremiah 1:6). I am too young! People will not take me seriously. I cannot be effective.

We are never too young to serve. We must not underrate our effectiveness. Youth is neither a handicap nor a shelter from responsibility.

Neither can we be too old. Remember Sarah's scepticism when her improbable pregnancy was foretold? "We are too old!" she said.

We may be too old for a certain physical feat, but we are never too old for new experiences or new challenges. Above all, we are never too old to learn, to teach and to serve.

"Too poor" strikes me as a particularly Terrible Too. Not very many people may say it; but many think it and act it. A paralyzing feeling of inferiority besets some financially handicapped persons. Their poverty engenders lack of self-respect and self-love. Many poor people think their poverty disqualifies them for service to the community or for a voluntary leadership role in the public arena. If you are poor, you may not be able to write a big cheque, but you can do many other generous things. You can do Mitzvot! You can be a model for others!

"Too rich."

No one will say these words, but the thought exists in some people's minds. Wealth is believed to exempt its owner from certain personal obligations, deemed to be beneath the status of affluence.

Of course, I know many well-to-do persons to whom this observation does not apply. Yet there is a disposition on the part of some wealthy individuals to be very generous with their substance, but to neglect, because of their affluence, the more humble Jewish and human duties: visiting the sick, comforting the mourners by personal attendance, or doing some of the less glamorous volunteer jobs in charitable organizations. "Let others do those things for me! I will take care of things more in my line!"

"Too weak!"

Often, it is not an excuse, but reality. Many people are too weak to resist any kind of temptation. They yield to nearly everything that might divert them from the pursuit of their objectives. Their lack of discipline prevents them from leading planned purposeful lives. They cannot study, because they cannot exercise the required self-control. They cannot reduce weight, because their will power is inadequate. They cannot "keep kosher," even if they wish, because a cheeseburger is too appetizing. They must cheat, because they cannot resist the temptation of quick gain.

135

Yet the most tragic of all the Terrible Too's is another one:

"Too busy."

"Too busy" is a universal affliction! Is there anyone who does not say "I'm too busy?" I know how often I use these words and how much I ought to preach to myself.

Unfortunately, when we say we are too busy it is not always a mere alibi, an empty excuse. It may be the truth; and that is even worse.

We make the mistake of allowing our work load to grow beyond limits. We combine working with other commitments, voluntary as well as obligatory ones, and we soon reach the sad state of being too busy.

Take my friend, the lawyer. He is busy in his office hours without end, not because he is greedy and tries to get as much business as he can, but simply because he is successful and his practice keeps growing. How can he turn his clients down? His reputation in the profession requires him to serve also as an officer in his professional organization; and how can he refuse to join the board of his condominium, or to be on the executive of a charitable cause he strongly supports?

We all know people whose tombstone should bear the epitaph: "He was too busy."

Some men are too busy to be fathers or husbands in a meaningful sense. Some women are too busy for the role of motherhood and family building. The same individuals, or others, are too busy for Synagogue and for Jewish observance. Their busy schedule does not allow for time to prepare a Seder, to build a Sukkah or to buy a Lulav.

Many of us are too busy to play. We all deserve a little time off, a chance to play golf or tennis, to keep physically fit, to enjoy recreation or the pleasure of travel.

On the other extreme, you find people who are so busy having fun, so busy travelling, so busy with sports or games, that they have no time for their children, their parents or their grandparents. Needless to say, they are too busy for friendship or love, for it takes time, precious time, to be a friend or to love another person in a meaningful way.

In the spirit of Yom Kippur, we could write a veritable confession of sins, a litany after the model of *"Al Chet Sheh-chatanu,"* on the theme of being too busy:

I have sinned for I was
> too busy to go to Shule;
>> too busy to watch my daughter performing in her school play;
>>> too busy to see my doctor;
>>>> too busy to make that phone call for my friend;
>>>>> too busy to visit my mother.

Heaven forbid!- but not until they sit on the ruins of their lives do some people realize they were busy with the unimportant, with the trivia that turned to dust. They were so busy that they had no time for the things which they recognize too late were the truly important part of their lives.

Too late, too late! The final, devastating Terrible Too!

There is a beautiful Midrash explaining why it was the prophet Isaiah who was chosen to bring comfort to the people Israel with his promises of redemption and restoration, far beyond the vision of any other prophet. It was *"because he accepted the yoke of heaven"* - God's mandate to become a prophet- *"with joy and alacrity"* (Tanna D'bei Eliyahu 16, quoted in Yalkut Shimeoni 408 on Isaiah 6:8).

In his vision, Isaiah saw God on his heavenly throne, surrounded by his attending angels; and he heard God's voice saying "Whom shall we send? Who will go for us?" And Isaiah answered *"Hin'ni shlacheini - here I am; send me!"* (Isaiah 6:8).

Isaiah offered no alibis. He did not say "I am too young!" "I am too tired!" "I am too busy!" He simply said: *"Hineini - Here I am!"*

The purpose of the Days of Awe is that we change.

Our aim is not to persuade God to comply with our will and thus gain control over God. Rather do we want to accept God's will, discipline ourselves, and give him control over our lives. If the Terrible Too's interfere with our good intentions, this is the day to break their tyranny!

May we leave behind the Terrible Too's and accept God's challenges with joy!

The Only Day

People move in different directions. Some get wiser, others more foolish. Some get richer, others poorer. Some get better, others move in the opposite direction and deteriorate.

One process we all undergo equally: we all get older. In this track, we all travel in the same direction. Everyone ages. It begins at birth and does not stop till we die.

A sermon on ageing is therefore always of topical interest, even more than a sermon on death. Our own death we can only imagine and usually we don't bother. Ageing we experience. It is an inescapable fact of life, of which we become increasingly aware as the years fly past.

In 1982 I had already passed enough milestones to be very empathetic with those who fear the coming of old age and resent the injuries and insults of the ageing process. An inscription on the base of an antique sundial makes this sorrowful comment on the passing hours:

"Each one wounds; the last one kills."

"Future shock" aggravates the hurt of ageing. Change has overtaken us with such speed that only the young who do not have to relearn old ways can be fully at home in the present. Ageing makes us not only older but obsolete.

The shrinking distance to retirement age had made me increasingly conscious of the challenge to accept ageing realistically and courageously. We must neither live in the past, as the years pile up on our shoulders, nor must we accept passively that life is a non-renewable resource.

Then I saw the film "On Golden Pond." It was the catalyst I needed to compose a sermon on ageing. I am grateful that my ideas have stood me in good stead.

I titled the sermon "The Only Day."

The Only Day ───────────────
A Sermon preached on Shabbat Vayechi 5743 - 1982

The film "On Golden Pond" chronicles a retired couple's summer at their lakeside cottage, from the lush awakening of the season to its fiery descent into fall. I found it to be a deeply moving portrayal of old age, its pathos and beauty, and of one person's rebellion against its inevitability.

The main character is the husband, a retired professor. He is a bitter, angry and sarcastic old man. No doubt, some of these traits were only deepened, but not engendered, by advancing years and retirement. His daughter's alienation from her father is clearly the result of being rebuffed by her father's critical nature during her formative years.

However, all his negative traits are exacerbated as a reaction to his decline. Age is the enemy. He has been shunted aside; he has to accept the indignity of increasing infirmity and the loss of faculties.

Every change is a reminder of death.

Then comes a turning point. The plot presents a surprise. Age admits the possibility of unexpected growth.

> *In old age they still produce fruit; they are full of sap*
> *and freshness (Psalm 92:15).*

The surprise comes from an unlikely source. The daughter shows up and parks her current boy friend's son of thirteen years with her parents so as to rid herself of this encumbrance. The old man starts out by resenting this selfish intrusion. Yet gradually, his feelings change. The young boy captures his heart and the two share a magic summer, full of wondrous experiences for both. The old man experiences a depth of personal emotion he had never felt before. Instead of sterility and desiccation, old age grants him new growth. The film culminates on a redemptive note: her father's new emotional capacity liberates his daughter's latent love for him and enables the two to break through the barriers of accumulated inhibitions.

Few of us are strangers to "birthday blues." We may have passed the 30-year or 40-year milestones, feared as signposts of precipitous decline. It is a typically modern trauma. Old age used to be venerated as an invaluable asset. In the Judaic tradition *"Zikna - Old Age,"* is equated with *"Chochma - wisdom,"* the accumulated experience of a lifetime which helps to cope with life. It makes the elder an inestimable resource in meeting life's problems. By contrast, moderns fear the ageing process and its intimations of approaching death. A veritable phobia of age poisons the middle years for many people.

The Torah portion assigned to this Shabbat portrays Jacob in his old age and recounts his death. It begins with the words: *"Jacob lived in the land of Egypt for seventeen years"* (Genesis 47:28).

The classical commentators point out that in the traditional Hebrew numerology, the number "17" is equivalent to the word *"Tov,"* which means *"good."* Despite illness, frailty and death, the years of Jacob's old age were good.

The narrative of Jacob's death begins with the word *"Vayechi - he lived."* We are to focus on life as long as we have it, in the present, rather than allow the dread of anticipated death to dilute the intensity of the present moment.

The terminality of life must not paralyze us.

We must live each day fully, not as if it was our *last*, but as if it was our *only one.*

How many yesterdays there were is irrelevant; how many tomorrows there will be, is immaterial. Live the present day as if it was all of life!

Is not each day a mini-life? Waking up is like birth, and going to sleep a little bit of death.

In between these daily terminals, life calls for enthusiasm, for boldness, for the courage of youth as well as for the experience and wisdom of age.

Each day I want to learn, to grow, to expand the horizon of the world I know. Each day I want to love and be loved. Each day I want to drink from the cup of victory, and bow down, if I must, to sip from the bowl of bitterness, for defeat and pain are the badge of my humanity. And each day I want to be for others, for that is the badge of my divinity. I want to give my best each day and make it unique and precious without regard to age, without being bound to the accumulating past and diminished by the dwindling expectation of future.

If I am not for myself, who is for me? If I am for myself,
what am I? And if not now, when? (Pirkei Avot 1:14).

It is the *"Now,"* the present day that is the essence of my life. We
have nothing else, nor do we need anything more.

Of course, I wish, I dream, I am nostalgic. "I wish I was twenty
years younger!" But I shall never be. I shall never be younger than
today. But today I was born. My day is new.

I cannot reverse directions. Life has no rewind. It is in each moment.
I am in the Here and Now.

So do not look back in nostalgia, nor ahead in paralyzing fear.
Experience in the present day the fullness of life; in fleeting time,
the presence of eternity!

The FOURTH *window*

The Bread of Brotherhood

On December 10, 1990, I enjoyed the privilege of participating in the Media Human Rights Awards Dinner of the League for Human Rights of B'nai Brith Canada. The special guest of honour was Rabbi Gunther Plaut who was being honoured for his outstanding contributions to the cause of human rights in Canada.

Rabbi Plaut had requested that I make the Invocation and "Hamotzee," the Blessing over the Bread.

Whenever I am asked to offer an invocation before a dinner, I try to use it to communicate a Jewish idea that relates both to the programmatic nature of the function and to the meal, so that I can end my words with the Hamotzee blessing. When I pondered the meaning of the Hamotzee on the occasion of the Human Rights Awards Dinner, I perceived in this blessing, in which we thank God for producing food "from the earth," an emphasis on the notion that God's creative power produces our food out of the inedible, indigestible soil.

Indeed, I discovered a relationship, a poetic one perhaps, between that idea and the purpose of the evening.

The Bread of Brotherhood ——————————
A Prayer at the Human Rights Awards Dinner of
B'nai Brith December 10, 1990

> *"Hamotzee lechem min ha-aretz - God brings forth bread from the earth."*

Touched by his creative spirit,
    through the chemistry of sun and rain and nutrients,
    the inert soil yields grain.

    Grain becomes flour
        and flour becomes our bread.

In a night of chaos
    a candle is lit
        and there is a gleam of light
            and light begets vision
                and vision turns to hope.

In the incoherent clutter of ignorance
    a creative thought is conceived,
        and thought engenders knowledge,
            and out of knowledge comes wisdom.

In a jumble of sound and fury
    an intelligent word sparks communication,
        and communication leads to understanding,
            and out of understanding comes friendship.

In a world of confusion
    there begins a search for clarity,
        and seeking leads to truth,
            and truth makes for justice,
                and justice brings peace.

O God. bless those who sow the seed,
        who light the candle,
    who think the thought,
        who utter the word,
            and who begin the search.

                And bless us all who break the
                bread together!

Baruch Atta ... Blessed art Thou, o Lord, King of the Universe, who brings forth food from the earth. Amen.

To Canada with Love

In the late 70's, an unexpected chain of events began to affect me. Voices from my distant past reopened chapters of my life I had long considered closed and reactivated dormant files of my personal chronology. A Catholic priest and a Protestant minister in my home town, Cologne-Mülheim, asked me for help with a joint project of their parishes: to research the vanished Jewish community of Mülheim and its history. As I found out subsequently, a renewed interest in the obliterated German-Jewish communities was making itself strongly felt throughout Germany.

Out of our ensuing correspondence grew mutual interest, involvement and friendship. Eventually, the Christian churches invited me to visit Mülheim. This community of about 50,000 was a century ago a separate municipality, located across from Cologne on the east bank of the Rhine. Today it is just a part of the expanding city.

My visit stirred a great deal of interest in the circles of the Toronto Christian community with whom I had been engaged in dialogue. They encouraged my extensive itinerary of teaching, consulting, speaking at both the Catholic and Protestant churches, and preaching at one unprecedented joint Sunday service. They regarded it as a Christian-German initiative toward reconciliation with the Jewish people. Christians in Toronto, who had devoutly hoped for closer Christian-Jewish relations, warmly welcomed the German initiative. On a more political level, the German consulate in Toronto and the German government in Bonn took favourable notice of my visit. Their interest resulted in a few additions to my German program, such as a briefing at the German Foreign Ministry in Bonn and visits to academic centres involved in Jewish studies.

My visit was very eventful and rewarding. It stirred deep feelings in all who became involved. It led to several further visits to Germany with interesting and fruitful results.

In recognition of my German outreach, I was proposed for the Human

Relations Award of the Canadian Council of Christians and Jews, one of the sponsors of the Christian-Jewish Dialogue of Toronto.

The Annual Dinner of the Canadian Council of Christians and Jews took place on December 2, 1981, very shortly after my return from my initial visit to Germany. I was still under its impact. I had fled from Germany as a persecuted Jew forty years earlier and now had been given a kind of hero's welcome! Under the spell of that experience and the conflicting emotions it had evoked in me, the presentation of the Human Relations Award was overwhelming, all the more so since I had the honour of making the response on behalf of the several recipients. For me, it was the thrilling culmination of an eventful year.

To Canada with Love
An Acceptance Address on Being Presented the HUMAN RELATIONS AWARD of the Canadian Council of Christians and Jews at the Annual Dinner on December 2, 1981

On behalf of the recipients of the Human Relations Award I would like to express our deep gratitude to the Canadian Council of Christians and Jews for bestowing on us such an honour.

Respect for truth compels me to disclaim the possession of any merit that would entitle me to this distinction.

Immodesty, on the other hand, permits me to say that the Award I received reflects my love for Canada and my concern for all her people. I regard the Human Relations Award as a confirmation of my hope to contribute to the development of a Canadian society that will achieve unity in diversity and will exemplify human dignity, decency and respect of tradition.

My love for Canada is nurtured by gratitude for the many opportunities that Canada offered me and for its many gifts to me, including my dear wife, Laura, born in Montreal.

I am happy that this evening concludes a great day in Canadian history, a day to make us proud to be Canadians. I am referring to the important vote held this afternoon in the House of Commons [1].

My love for Canada was deepened by my recent visit to the city of my birth, Cologne, Germany. I visited Germany in response to an invitation from German Christians who had asked me to help them come to terms with their past. They wanted to confront their share of responsibility for the history of the Nazi period and the crimes commissioned and perpetrated by Germany.

They felt I could offer them guidance to understand the dimensions of the tragedy that had so profoundly affected my life, and that I would be able to focus their perspective on collective responsibility and institutional guilt.

I want you to know I did my very best. Painful though it was, I told the story of my childhood and youth over and over again to different audiences. I talked about my parents, my friends, and their individual tragedies. I was able to convey to my listeners, especially to the younger ones who are puzzled by the notion of Jewish Germans, a sense of the past in real human terms. It was a fantastic experience for them to converse with someone who seemed to come out of history, yet who had lived right in their community and had walked the same streets as they. It boggled their mind.

I talked at length about Canada. I explained to them the concept of the Canadian mosaic, a concept which fascinated them and suggested to them a new approach to variety in human society.

I talked to them about Judaism and about the Jewish people. I tried my best to explain Jewish values, and how they appear in our tradition and in our teaching.

They could not get enough. Some individuals, especially among my younger listeners, related to me with an intensity that was almost embarrassing.

"What will I do without you?" exclaimed a young Christian minister who had followed me to each one of my engagements with the loyalty of a disciple to his master.

One reason for my being received with such concentrated attention is the pathetic absence of Jews in Germany. Hitler achieved one of his major objectives: he deprived Germany of the Jewish presence. Christians who want to dialogue with Jews cannot find dialogue partners; students who want to learn first-hand how Jews define themselves cannot find Jewish teachers. There are societies for Christian-Jewish cooperation, and councils for interfaith dialogues and relationships, but not enough Jews to participate. There are hardly any survivors of the old Jewish community that was so integrated into the spiritual and cultural life of Germany. The few thousand Jews who live in Cologne today are mostly newcomers. Their roots are not in Germany. They have shared few, if any, experiences with their German contemporaries. They cannot relate to Germans on the level of meaningful self-disclosing dialogue, nor do they have much desire to do so.

Imagine the resulting emotional turbulence! Christians conversing with ghosts, with an accusatory absence created by the diabolical crime of genocide that was perpetrated by their parents and grandparents and -what hurts them most- tolerated by the religious institutions which they love!

These emotional tensions accounted for the intensity of my experience and for the nature of the attachments my visit created. "Would you come back and live here again?" they asked me. "At least come back soon to speak to us again!" "Please come back often!"

After this experience, I can only love Canada more and give thanks. How grateful we ought to be for the opportunities we enjoy to talk to one another, to share together, to argue, to disagree, to cooperate and to love!

This gratitude compels us to work together for a great Canada. We must build a country that incorporates the best of our shared values: a society characterized by a humanism that is based on spiritual values and on the awareness that we are accountable to our Creator for this country and for the welfare of its people!

How sad it would be if the bitter experiences suffered in the past were to persuade us to withdraw from this endeavour! How lamentable if the burdens of our history, the humiliations we endured and the disappointments we bore, were to inhibit our capacity to hope, so that we would turn away in anger or despair. Yes, it would be understandable, but very sad.

In the Book of Exodus, among the instructions Moses received for the building of the Sanctuary, we find a description of the two "Cherubim," angelic figures made of gold that were to be placed on the cover of the Ark of the Covenant.

The two angels were to be positioned so that they appeared to be looking at each other. "...*their faces turning each to his brother*" (Exodus

25:20), is the literal translation of the Hebrew text. That verse seems to contradict a passage in the Book of Chronicles where we find a description of the Sanctuary which specifies that the Cherubim are to face the interior of the building (II Chronicles 3:13).

The Talmud (Baba Batra 99a) resolves the contradiction by positing the regular occurrence of a miracle: as long as the people of Israel obeyed God's commands, the Cherubim's faces were turned to each other; when the people were unfaithful, the angels averted their faces from each other and turned their gaze to the interior of the building.

May I propose that the Talmudic sages were not necessarily describing a supernatural miracle. Their explanation may not imply that the golden figures were really able to shift from one position to another. Suppose that the gold angels were fixed in an intermediate position, partly looking at each other and partly turned to the interior! Their orientation would then depend on the perception of the beholder. If the beholder wanted to see brotherliness and a posture of mutual caring, he could; if he wanted to perceive isolation and withdrawal, he could too.

In our religious traditions, we find elements of distinctiveness, of inwardness and exclusivity. There are moments for turning our faces to the interior of our sanctuaries. But we also find strong elements of universality; times for gazing at our brothers and sisters, opportunities of reaching out to others. There are values that are meant to be shared; there are goals that can be realized only through relationships with other human beings; there are incentives to strive for universal brotherhood, and ideals that challenge us to rise above parochial differences.

Whether we emphasize the elements of distinctiveness or those of communality is our choice. Faithfulness to God, our Sages seem to suggest, means looking at one another. Obedience to Him demands turning to our brothers and sisters and assuming the attitude of brotherhood and of communality. God's mandate is to face our brothers, not to turn away from them.

Judaism and Christianity share the vision of a great Messianic hope. Jewish and Christian hearts wait for the coming of a new universal order that will bring unity and solidarity to the people of the world. We dream of an era of justice and peace and universal love, when the lion will lie down with the lamb and no creature will hurt another.

151

Can it be wrong to grow dissatisfied with waiting passively for that ideal time to come? Can it be wrong to start working for the achievements of these ideals in the here and now, not leaving them for a utopian future? Should we not display a divine impatience with all the obstacles, such as ignorance, backwardness, prejudice and hate, that stand in the way of making the vision a reality?

So let us turn our faces to one another, Ladies and Gentlemen, and let us work together for knowledge, for fairness, for justice, for love and for peace!

---

[1] *On December 2, 1981, the Canadian House of Commons passed by an overwhelming majority a resolution to repatriate the British North America Act.*

The First Zionist

It is a paradox that the Conservative Movement in Judaism which was committed to Zionism since its very inception did not launch a Zionist organization until the 1980's.

Conservative Jews were members and leaders in a wide spectrum of Zionist organizations and therefore did not feel the need for a Zionist entity within the corporate structure of the Conservative Movement.

Eventually, it became obvious that the lack of a Zionist organization deprived Conservative Judaism of an effective political arm within the structure of the World Zionist Movement. In Israel the evolving Conservative community was handicapped by its failure to achieve recognition as an authentic stream within religious Judaism. The Conservative rabbinate was hurt and incensed by the refusal of the religious authorities in Israel to recognize Conservative Rabbis as legitimate and to allow them to carry out Rabbinic functions.

As a result, "Mercaz" came into being. "Mercaz" means "centre" or "focus" in Hebrew. In English, the name is an acronym for "Movement to Reaffirm Conservative Zionism."

The development of "Mercaz" was accelerated by the persistent efforts of orthodox political parties in Israel to amend the Law of Return. The proposed amendment to exclude Conservative converts to Judaism from the definition of Jews was seen as an attempt to delegitimize the Conservative Rabbinate, and thus the entire movement. The general willingness of other political parties to support this amendment if it was politically expedient drove home the point to Conservative Jews that "Mercaz" was needed.

The 31st World Zionist Congress, held in Jerusalem in 1987, was a further incentive to mobilize Conservative Jews for "Mercaz."

"Mercaz Canada" evolved in conjunction with the "Canadian Council for Conservative Judaism (CCCJ)." I served as president of Mercaz Canada during the first two years of its existence, and was privileged to represent it as a delegate at the Zionist Congress.

153

My commitment to Mercaz is founded on the hope that Conservative Judaism may help bring about a religious reawakening in Israel and inspire a renewal of Zionist idealism. Many secular Israelis feel a spiritual hunger. There is a yearning for a Jewish tradition that can be blended with modernity and democracy. For this reason, a movement rooted in tradition, with an emphasis on ethics and based on a Halacha that embraces the realities of a modern pluralistic Jewish society is one of Israel's greatest needs.

In a sermon a few months before my departure for Jerusalem, I tried to develop my vision of Zionism as a dual road to Jewish reformation. Based on a Midrashic comment, this sermon depicts our patriarch Isaac as the prototype of Zionism.

The First Zionist
A sermon preached on Parshat Toldot 5748 - 1987

אל תרד מצרימה שכן בארץ...
עשה שכונה בארץ ישראל
הוי זורע הוי נוטע. דבר אחר:
שכן את השכינה בארץ

> The Lord appeared to him and said: "Do not go down to Egypt! Dwell in the Land ..." (Genesis 26:2)

> Dwell in the Land means: "Make a dwelling in the land of Israel: sow! plant!" Another interpretation: "Prepare a dwelling for God's presence in the Land"

> (Midrash Rabba 64).

Our ancestor Isaac was the only one of our patriarchs never to live outside the Land of Israel.

His father Abraham had been born in Mesopotamia and did not hesitate, when famine threatened, to leave the promised land for greener pastures in Egypt. His son Jacob founded family and fortune in Aramean exile and spent the last years of his life in Egypt.

154

Not so our patriarch Isaac.

The experience of the "Akeda," of being bound as a sacrifice on the altar, the knife raised over his neck, had conferred on him unique sanctity. Spared from martyrdom only by grace of supernatural intervention, he was not to tarnish his holiness by leaving the Land. When he wanted to follow his father's example and wait out a famine in Egypt, God countermanded his intention:

"Do not go down to Egypt! Sh'chon ba-aretz - dwell in the land!" (Genesis 26:3).

We are all Isaacs. We are all survivors, who escaped from the knife. If, Heaven forbid, Germany had not been defeated in World War II, not one of us would be alive today. At the Wannsee Conference, so graphically recreated in a recent German film, the Nazi leadership made the decision to exterminate all Jews, everywhere.

The remnant of the Jewish people, especially of European Jewry, reacted to the Holocaust with tenacious resolve. There was only one land where survivors could live: the land of Israel. Thus, the State of Israel rose from the ruins of the European communities and new life was born out of the ashes of the Holocaust.

We are Isaacs even if we do not live in Israel now. Having come so close to destruction, we all belong to a consecrated generation.

The Zionist idea -that Jews must be sovereign on their own land- must therefore be the central feature of our ideological landscape. The imperative *"Dwell in the land!"* addressed originally to Isaac, is addressed to us as well: we are to be a Jewish nation on the only Jewish land there is in the world.

Isaac was the first Zionist.

The land had been promised to his father, Abraham: *To your descendants will I give this land (Genesis 12:7).* Abraham, the man of faith, believed in the promise, not unlike many generations of pious Jews in Exile who were comforted and heartened by a promise of redemption even though they saw no sign of its fulfillment. They were prepared to wait for its fulfilment through divine intervention.

Thus, when Abraham needed land for a burial ground, he had to negotiate and to plead with the Hittite owners of the land.

For Abraham, God's promise to give his descendants the land remained only a promise, nothing more.

155

Isaac was different. A mere promise, no matter how deep his faith, was not enough. When God repeated the promise to him and commanded him *"Sh'chon ba-aretz - dwell in the land,"* he took the word *"sh'chon"* to mean *"assei sh'chuna b'eretz yisrael - establish a 'Shechuna,' a settlement, in the Land of Israel! Sow! Plant!"* (Breishit Rabba 64). He tilled the soil, he planted, he sowed. He was the first of his nomadic family to engage in agriculture and to settle on the land. A mere promise could not satisfy him. He had to implement the promise with his own hands!

That is what Zionism was all about.

The early proponents of Zionism insisted that the Jewish situation had become untenable. In Russia, where Jews had not assimilated, they reeled from pogroms fuelled by implacable brutal hatred. In France, the enlightened, cultured cradle of human rights, where Jews were emancipated, integrated and acculturated, the Dreyfus Trial had shown the deeply rooted anti-Semitism of the nation.

For Zionists, the message was clear: only a national home could make Jews into a normal people, living like all other peoples, on their own soil. Nothing else could solve the Jewish problem.

The vision was preposterous, a fairy tale, a utopian dream. A Jewish commonwealth, no less!

Most Western Jews were inclined to reject the Zionist message. They agreed with the position of Reform Judaism that Judaism was a religion, not a nationality. Jews were not a people in the modern meaning of the term. They were Germans, Frenchmen, British who happened to be Jewish.

Orthodox Jews, on the other hand, who did believe in Jewish peoplehood, were apt to oppose "self-redemption" as an act of rebellion against God's governance. They believed in the promise, like Abraham, and had faith that God's Messiah would bring redemption in God's own time, but to preempt the divine timetable through action, through Zionist settlement in the Land of Israel, was to defy God's will.

The Zionists, however, followed Isaac. *"Establish a settlement in the Land of Israel: sow! plant!"* In other words, the promise requires our efforts for its fulfillment.

Thus, Chalutzim went on Aliya. They drained the swamps and

planted in the wilderness while the political leaders of Zionism negotiated with the powers of the world.

Fifty years after the First Zionist Congress, the political and the pioneering streams of Zionism flowed together and culminated in the creation of Israel.

Do you remember November 29, 1947? The United Nations Assembly was voting on the partition of Palestine and the creation of a Jewish State. A positive vote required a two-third majority. While the powers of the world cajoled and arm-twisted, we devoured the press and sat glued to the radio. Without the consent of the United Nations, no Jewish state would come into being. The world had to give its permission.

That was the last time. That was the last time that our fate would be decided by the nations of the world. The last time. No more! We became a sovereign people, making our own decisions, right or wrong, wise or foolish. Jews determine Jewish fate! That is Zionism.

But Zionism is more.

The Midrash offers a second interpretation of *"Sh'chon ba-aretz -dwell in the land." "Shakkein et hash'china ba-aretz - make a dwelling place for the 'Shechina,' God's presence, in the land!"* Isaac's settlement was to be the home of the Divine.

Zionism is not merely reaction to anti-Semitism and the Holocaust. It goes beyond the physical and political restoration of the Jewish people.

Judaism and Zionism are inseparable.

Without a state, without a society of its own to bring the Jewish ethos down to earth, Judaism lacks reality.

Yet without a commitment to Jewish spiritual and moral values, a state cannot be the homeland of the Jewish people and the instrument of its redemption.

For this reason, the State of Israel and the Jewish people need Zionism that is based on our religious tradition. While I speak for Conservative Zionism, I believe that other religious movements may make similar claims. The Masorti Movement, as Conservative Judaism is called in Israel, and Mercaz, the Zionist organization created by the Conservative Movement, are dedicated to the creation of a moral, just and compassionate Israeli society, whose spirituality springs from the sources of Torah and Jewish tradition.

The process of creating such a society has a strong impact on Judaism as well. Judaism itself is changed, renewed and revitalized, when it is compelled to confront the full range of societal issues in the context of a modern state. The ancient model of Judaism was that of an authoritarian system, enforced through social and legal coercion. The democratic nature of a modern Jewish society, however, mandates a pluralistic model, a system under which religious commitment is not enforced and regulated by the state and by public law, but which encourages voluntary spiritual and religious choices made by individuals and by groups.

Not by virtue of historical associations, only by virtue of the moral and spiritual quality of the life of her people, can the Land of Israel merit the name "Holy Land" and Jews the title "Holy People."

The Jewish people has fulfilled the first half of Isaac's mandate. The "Shechuna," the tangible settlement, has been established. The second half, the home of the "Shechina," remains to be created.

Zionism so understood is neither obsolete nor rendered superfluous by the State of Israel. Its goals are yet to be achieved; its ideals are still to be defined and realized.

We all are Isaac. We have escaped from the sword and survived the gas chambers. Like Isaac's, the home of our ideals must forever remain the Zionist vision.

Is There Life After Death?

Since the dawn of conscience, the hope that human existence continues after death has nourished the roots of religions. The Royal pyramids of ancient Egypt and the New Age practice of "channelling" are manifestations of the same quest for immortality that began when the human mind learned to grasp notions of life, death, time and continuity.

Life after death occupies a prominent part in the teaching of Judaism. It is, however, one of the traditional doctrines that have become problematic in an enlightened scientific age. Moreover, the thrust of religious policy in the post-war era did not encourage concentration on the other-worldly concerns of religion. Social, economic and political issues were deemed more worthy of the attention of Church and Synagogue than speculation about the afterlife. The Here and Now crowded out the Hereafter.

In the last decade, the pendulum has swung again in the direction of spirituality and mysticism. Rationalism has had its day and was found wanting. It was unable to satisfy the spiritual thirst that the majority of religious people sought to satisfy at the wellsprings of their faith.

As the date of my anticipated retirement was looming closer, I felt the need to devote sermons to fundamental questions of faith that I had not discussed adequately before. I decided to preach on the last Yom Kippur before my retirement on the question "Is There Life After Death?"

Is There Life After Death?
A Sermon preached on Yom Kippur 5749 - 1988
before Yizkor

The first prayer traditionally taught to Jewish children was the *"Modeh Ani."*

Perhaps your parents, your grandparents, or a Nursery School teacher, taught it to you.

159

מוֹדֶה אֲנִי לְפָנֶיךָ מֶלֶךְ חַי וְקַיָּם
שֶׁהֶחֱזַרְתָּ בִּי נִשְׁמָתִי בְּחֶמְלָה

I give thanks before You, living and everlasting King,
for giving me back my soul in mercy; great is
Your faithfulness. (Siddur)

"Modeh Ani" is to be recited on awakening. It does not mention the word "God" or his Holy Name so that you may recite it while still in bed, before you have washed your hands.

Repeated every morning, this prayer taught the child important religious and moral concepts, for instance, to say "Thanks." Above all it introduced the child to an essential idea, the idea of a soul, the "Neshama."

The simple prayer offers no precise philosophical definitions. The presence of the soul is the difference between being awake and asleep. Without it, I am a clod, mere flesh; breathing; but without consciousness, judgement, control, or deliberate thought.

The child thus grew up with the awareness that we have a soul. We depend on God to guard it while we are asleep and to return it to us each morning. We need not worry, for we may count on His faithfulness.

Eventually, as the child progressed to more advanced prayers, a more elaborate theology of the soul evolved in the *"Elohay Neshama":*

> *O God, the soul You have given me is pure; You created it, You fashioned it, and You breathed it into me. You guard it within me. You will reclaim it from me in time to come, but only to restore it to me in the ultimate future.* (Siddur)

In this prayer, recited daily in private devotion before the formal Blessings of the Morning, we encounter more elaborate ideas about the soul. It is the divine part within me, pure and untainted. It is entrusted to me by God, who made me responsible for keeping it immaculate until he will take it back from me. Not forever, though; at the appointed time-to-come, my self will be reconstituted through the restoration of my soul.

Clearly, this prayer reflects and teaches belief in Resurrection.

160

Three times every day, four times on Shabbat, and five times on Yom Kippur, we recite in the second blessing of the "Amida" the following lines:

> *You feed the living in lovingkindness; You revive the dead in your abundant mercy. You support the fallen; You heal the sick and release the prisoners. You are trusted faithfully to revive the dead. Blessed are You, o Lord, Who revive the dead.*

We say God sustains the helpless, the fallen, the sick, the prisoners, and among them the most helpless of all, the dead. They are not beyond the range of God's loving and constant concern.

Maimonides states as the 13th principle of our faith, *"I believe with perfect faith that there will be a resurrection of the dead at the time when it shall please the Creator, blessed be His Name."*

Do we require more examples to demonstrate that classical Judaism believes in Immortality?

True, our tradition offers many diverse teachings on the subject of the afterlife. The teachings often appear to be discrepant, inconsistent. They are difficult to reconcile. There is the theme, with several variations, of the survival of the soul after death; the expectation of reward and punishment; the theory of purification through "Gehinnom," a state of punishment, and of reward in "Gan Eden," spiritual or even sensual bliss in paradise; and also the idea of Resurrection.

Such popular customs as Kaddish, Yizkor and Yortzeit are based on belief in an afterlife.

Our Sages caution us against too literal an interpretation of all these notions. The afterlife is unknowable, indescribable and totally beyond our experience. The descriptions found in our tradition are not to be taken literally, for *"no eye has ever seen it, except you, o God"* (Isaiah 64:3).

However, the ancient Rabbis never wavered in their belief in immortality. Death is not the end of the human existence. It is not the beginning of nothingness.

They might well agree with Rabindranath Tagore who wrote: *"Death is not extinguishing the light; it is putting out the lamp because the dawn has come"* (quoted in "A Treasury of Comfort," ed. Sidney Greenberg).

This life is preparation for eternity. It is our chance to affect the quality of the afterlife. Its consequences are forever.

Science and modern skepticism have all but demolished belief in an afterlife. In the absence of evidence, our notion of immortality may be merely wishful thinking. It reflects our yearning for permanence. The fact that belief in an afterlife is so universal attests not the objective truth of this doctrine, but to the universality and tenacity of the basic human need to believe it.

The emphasis on the afterlife in so much of our classical literature is therefore embarrassing for many contemporary Jewish teachers. They prefer the thesis that Judaism emphasizes our commitment to this world and to this life, rather than to a life after death. Our task is not to speculate about the Hereafter, but to make the present world a paradise.

Perhaps a little too smugly, rabbis often contrast the Jewish emphasis on our responsibility for this world and the Christian accent on "the other world." Suffer here, promises the Christian ethos, and enjoy later! Judaism, on the other hand, encourages us to try to improve this world, as if there was no other, and leave the rest to God.

Few Jewish sermons ever deal affirmatively with the subject of the afterlife. I feel as if I myself had been part of a "conspiracy of silence," for I have never devoted an entire sermon to this topic, except in the context of highlighting the "this-worldly" emphasis of Judaism.

Not that the "this-worldliness" of Judaism is a modern fabrication. It is true that Judaism sharpens our responsibility for our life on this earth. Judaism disparages the inclination of religious saints, whose faith assures them of eternal bliss in the world beyond, to ignore or accept the evil of the Here and Now.

Yet Judaism has never denied the truth of immortality and individual survival.

In support of the "this-worldly" attitude of Judaism, modern Jewish teachers love to quote Pirke Avot: *"One hour of Repentance and good deeds in this world is better than the whole life of the world to come"* (Avot 4:22).

It is dishonest, though, to quote only the first half of this statement and to omit conveniently the second half which reads: *"... yet better is one hour of bliss in the next world than the whole life of this world!"*

To omit the second half of this beautiful paradox completely changes its meaning!

Last Fall, my Synagogue presented a Lecture series on the Jewish approach to death and afterlife.

It attracted unusually large crowds. "Why," I was asked, "should so serious a subject as death and the afterlife command such popularity?"

In reply I quoted the question that a puzzled fund-raiser once asked the wise Rabbi. "Why is it so much easier to raise money for a hospital than for an academy of higher Jewish learning? Why is a wealthy benefactor more inclined to write a big cheque for a hospital than for a Yeshivah?"

"Simple!" replied the Rabbi. "The wealthy patron knows that, being human, even he is liable to suffer serious illness one day and to require the services of a hospital. That he may some day become a scholar and require an institution of higher learning – that he does not anticipate!"

What lies beyond life and death is a question that affects all of us. It is therefore an important topic.

I was prompted to break my silence on the subject when I recently attended a Shabbat service at a Reconstructionist Synagogue. It struck me how all references to an individual afterlife had been carefully purged from the text of the traditional prayers. Not that I was surprised. I knew that the naturalistic theology of Reconstructionism demanded the exclusion of promises of immortality from the prayer book.

But then I thought, "This is unfair! Hardly anyone at this Service, except for the Rabbi, realizes that the original text of the prayers has been tampered with; that excisions have been made from the traditional text used for nearly 2000 years. Without even a footnote to indicate the alteration, this is a surreptitious deprivation of hope! Why should the worshippers not be told that before the Reconstructionist emendations, this prayer expressed the certainty of life beyond death?"

Do I believe in life after death?

I am not certain, but I am opposed to the embezzlement of a deep and meaningful hope. It is dishonest to allege or imply that Judaism does not offer this hope or does not admit this possibility.

Why deprive people of the hope that death is not final?

The Talmud (Sanhedrin 91a), recording a debate between one of the Sadducees, who denied immortality, and one of the Sages, preserves this striking argument: *"If those who never lived before, live, should not those who did live before, live again?"*

Life itself is miraculous. Coming into being is a mystery. The existence of the cosmos is an enigma; and so is my experience of my own self. How did I come into being? How did I become I?

Would life after death be any more miraculous?

The emergence of being from non-being is beyond the capacity of human reason. How can we, and why should we, categorically dismiss the possibility of an afterlife, of resurrection, or of the immortality of the individual?

Must we accept that nothing of us remains? Must we concede that He Who gave us life once cannot do so again? Must we surrender the hope of being reunited with those who preceded or will follow us?

Jewish thoughts about the afterlife are comforting, spiritual and uplifting.

Our hopes for eternity belong to the noblest expressions of the human spirit and of our kinship to the eternal God who created us.

Belief in an afterlife heightens our sense of meaning. If our prospect is nothingness, what is the point of responsibility or duty? Nonsense! Grab all you can and give nothing back!

If our lives are only a brief flash between "not yet" and "no more," meaning will be hard to find. But if I believe that my soul waited an eternity to be born and may leave this life enriched for another eternity to come, then there is a rationale for sacrifice, effort, self-denial. For life then holds the seed of eternity.

We may confess ignorance; we don't know. Yet we also may confess hope that our dear ones are still "there," that we can reach out to them; we can still be blessed by them - and they by us!

We confess the hope, perhaps too human, too naive, too much like the child's *"Modeh Ani,"* that in some fashion we shall see one another again sharing a bliss that with our earthbound imagination we could never envision.

My Personal Holocaust Remembrance

Two events dominate Jewish history in our century: the Holocaust and the rise of the State of Israel. It would not be an exaggeration to say that these were the two most important events of the Jewish millennium.

The State of Israel has remained centre stage. It makes headline news, yields reams of press copy and supports full television coverage. The State of Israel is Jewish history in the present tense.

The Holocaust is past tense. But it is not behind us. It is the background against which current events affecting Jews take place. We remain in its shadow.

At first, during the early post-war years, there was silence. No public voice spoke about the Holocaust. Survivors felt betrayed. Rabbis were frustrated. I remember Prof. Abraham Heschel, at a Rabbinical convention, confronting the terrible silence. "We are like orphans between the death and the funeral," he said. "We have not started to sit Shiv'a yet."

And then, the first voices were heard. Books appeared. Survivors spoke. Jews began to probe the past. First hesitantly, and then with increasingly shattering awareness, they ventured to the brink of the abyss.

The voices became a chorus. The initial trickle of publications became a torrent that has not abated until this day. Holocaust observances became a prominent feature of Jewish life. Holocaust studies turned into a rapidly proliferating branch of the Jewish curriculum on every level. The Holocaust became a point of departure for Jewish policy making and for creating a new relationship with the non-Jewish world.

Synagogues have been leading protagonists of Holocaust remembrance and study. As a sermon topic, the Holocaust is inexhaustible.

In recent years, two antithetical problems have surfaced. One is the danger that the Holocaust may be forgotten after the last survivors will have passed from the scene. Holocaust denial may become acceptable. Six million victims will be betrayed.

The other problem is the risk of making the Holocaust the ultimate rationale of Jewish life and commitment. Auschwitz may become the fountainhead of a macabre Judaism, the black hole that gives access to a bizarre world of spiritual anti-matter.

In the course of the years, I have preached many sermons on the Holocaust.

"My Personal Holocaust Remembrance," was my keynote address at a Holocaust Remembrance Service in Saskatoon in 1991. It had evolved from an address I presented at a meeting of the Tripartite Liaison Committee, an interfaith body which includes the Canadian Jewish Congress, in Ottawa on January 8, 1990.

My Personal Holocaust Remembrance —————
Keynote Address at the Holocaust Remembrance Service in Saskatoon on April 14, 1991

In the fall of 1988, an important speaking engagement took me to my native city, Cologne, Germany. I arrived tired after the long flight. Early in the evening my hosts took me to my quarters at the Jewish Retirement Home so that I might rest and recover from jet lag and be ready for my commitments the next day.

But I could not go to sleep. A strange restlessness had come over me. No sooner had I unpacked my suitcase than I slipped out into the dark streets. An anonymous stranger whom no one knew, I looked for the streetcar stop.

Twenty minutes later, having crossed the Rhine to the east bank, I arrived in Cologne-Mülheim, the suburb where I was born and where I had lived the first 18 years of my life. I walked about the dark streets as if drawn by some magnetic force or pushed on by an inner compulsion.

I crossed the square in front of the Church as I had done every day as a youth on my way to school. I passed the corner where my father's shoe store had stood fifty years ago. I passed the barber shop, the candy lady, and a site, now occupied by an ugly intruder, a shabby multiple dwelling. Here once stood my parental home.

167

What compels me to make this prowling pilgrimage, to yield to this furtive fling of nocturnal nostalgia?

In my heart I know. I know why I discreetly inspect the face of every passer-by. I know why my feet take me past the homes of the people I knew as a child.

I am looking for the vanished friends of my childhood.

I pass the house that was once the home of the Mohl family, pious, good German Jews, a well-to-do family, very observant and generous people. Herr Mohl was a good German patriot, proud of his service in the First World War.

Their four children, Heinz, Walter, Hanna and Martha, were my playmates, my childhood chums and my teenage buddies.

Not even one of them survived; not even one reached maturity. I suspect that in this whole wide world, no one else has ever mentioned them in public or told their story, and neither can I. For they are vanished like smoke out of a chimney, without a trace, without a monument, without a memory - and I don't know their story.

But talk about them I must; I must search for them, even on this obviously futile memory walk through the streets on which we once walked together and the parks in which we played. I must let my imagination speculate.

Where did Heinz draw his last breath?

When did Walter's heart beat the last time?

Which of the thousand faces of cruel death did beautiful Hanna see?

And before Martha died, at 17 or 18 years of age, what was her last thought about the goodness of life, the goodness of the world and of God?

Lithuania has been prominent in the news of late. Two years ago, there came to light a 1,700-page document, recording the fate of the Jews of Lithuania during the Holocaust. It had been compiled by a man, Leibl Koniuchowsky, now retired in Florida [1]. A Holocaust survivor himself, he held a government position in Lithuania after the war, and took advantage of the mobility it afforded him to interview other survivors. He collected the testimony of 153 Jews and detailed the destruction of the smaller Jewish communities in Lithuanian towns, including the burial places of the victims and the names of the criminals responsible for their deaths. Asked what motivated him to devote years to this pursuit, he answered: "I did what I did because it was an order from those who were taken away to die. They would look back and shout, 'Please remember us! Please don't forget!'"

"Forget me not!" is the plea of millions of individuals and of thousands of communities. "Don't forget how we died. Don't forget how we lived. For if you forget, we die over and over again."

Out of this psychological need to tell and obligation to remember, there has grown, and continues to grow, a tremendous enterprise.

The Holocaust has generated a flood of literature, fiction and history, a plethora of films and plays, and reams of theological and philosophical debate. Legal issues have arisen from attempts to bring Holocaust criminals to justice and to protect the integrity of historical truth.

Holocaust studies and research flourish in the academic world and appear on the curriculum of many institutions of learning.

Yet important as all that is, the most essential obligation is to create an emotional and intellectual awareness of the Holocaust in every human being and particularly in every Jew. The Holocaust must become part of the Jewish consciousness, inculcated in part through participation in regular remembrance observances and by institutionalizing "Yom Hasho'a" as the day for such observances.

Soon there will be no survivors left in our midst. There will a growing risk of forgetting, distorting, minimizing and mythologizing the Holocaust.

One danger is to downgrade its uniqueness and to speak of other disasters as "Holocausts," thus insinuating a comparability. We hear such expressions as "Holocaust of the Trees," or "Holocaust in Kuwait."

We must insist that the Holocaust is an enigma; that it is mysterious, unique, incomprehensible and unprecedented. It defies rational understanding. It bursts out of the frame of normal historical experience.

The Holocaust is in a class by itself for the Jewish people, no matter how long the Jewish litany of woes. It is *"sui generis"* for humanity

169

as a whole, without precedent in its interminable chronicle of slaughter and atrocity.

The Nazi method of killing Jews did not consist of inciting spontaneous pogroms or massacres by riotous mobs. No; it was a sophisticated program of genocide, the methodical extermination of an entire people.

It was an action aimed specifically and uniquely at Jews. Jews were not the only victims of the Nazis, but they were the only ones killed without ulterior pretext or without allegation of any crime, but simply for being Jews.

Being a Jew carried the death penalty.

It was a program of murder, planned systematically with the involvement of every establishment of the State and its various agencies: the Nazi party, law, education, business, science, religion and the media. All combined to prepare, plan and execute this program of genocide.

This, in all of human history, had never happened before.

Germany was a paragon of Western civilization. It was renowned for its cultural advancement, boasting a pantheon of philosophers, musical geniuses, poets, scientists. How could this nation, in the vanguard of every progressive movement, plan and execute the extermination of an entire people, with unspeakable brutality and with horrible acts of torture on a massive scale, and succeed to the extent of killing six million men, women and children?

And how could this program of extermination proceed under wartime conditions? How could it be given priority over military considerations, even though it syphoned off desperately needed war materiel and transport? How could it be more important for Germany to kill Jews than to win the war?

And how could millions of Germans, Poles, Ukrainians, Estonians and Lithuanians stand by averting their eyes while they tolerated, or participated in, what was being done?

And how could the whole world be spectators, disregarding the evidence, pretending ignorance and failing to intervene or even to raise a firm voice of protest?

That was unique. There is no parallel; there is no comparison. That had never happened before.

Eli Wiesel considers the Holocaust as the turning point, the watershed of human history. "After Auschwitz, the human condition is no longer the same. After Treblinka, nothing will ever be the same. The event has altered man's perception and changed his relationship to God, to his fellow man and to himself."

This year, forty-six years later, we observe the remembrance of the Holocaust against a background of fundamental changes in the world.

Two generations have grown up in the interval. We have seen the rise and fall of the Communist empire.

Much as we applaud the liberation, we are also horrified that all the traditional hatreds and antagonisms have come again to the surface.

The most sinister, the most threatening and ominous phenomenon of all is the revival of anti-Semitism that accompanies the revolutions in Eastern Europe.

These circumstances lend added importance and urgency to Holocaust remembrance. We must go on record once and for all that hatred of Jews is a horrible disease, associated with absolute evil.

Holocaust remembrance must reinforce our resolve to prevent genocidal violence in the future. Never again! Therefore, no one, anywhere, at any time, can acquiesce to anti-Semitism or tolerate it.

"Never again!" is a powerful slogan. We must remember history, it declares, lest we be condemned to repeat it. We must remember what were the calamitous results of moral indifference, of misplaced values, of faulty theology and of political cowardice. We must remember so that these mistakes will never again be repeated.

"Never again" must not be distorted to mean "They did it to us; so now we don't care if we do it to them." That would be a tragic betrayal of the martyrdom of our people.

"Never again!" must not mean "Never again to us!" but "Never again to anyone if we can help it!" Despite our terrible experiences, we must not allow ourselves to become petrified in the shape of perpetual victims and frozen in the sterility of permanent self-righteous anger.

We do not honour the memory of our martyred millions by becoming insensitive to the suffering of others. A week does not pass without my remembering my parents and my friends who perished in the Holocaust. I mourn for their cruelly abridged lives. But I would not bring honour to their memory by playing the role of the perpetual victim, hardened, defensive, uncompromising and always angry.

We cannot eradicate hatred by more hatred. True, we must bring Holocaust criminals to justice and fearlessly expose hate mongers. But beyond that, we must be personally involved in striving for understanding through education, dialogue and openness. Hatred cannot wipe out hatred. Only love and understanding can.

We must not stop at the question, "How could the world stand by? How could God allow it?" The brave, relevant, courageous question is, "How can we today tolerate injustice, racism, ethnic hatred and callous indifference to oppression and persecution wherever it may be found?"

"Never again" means commitment not only to remembering the past but also commitment to working for the future.

"Never again" demands our unswerving, uncompromising commitment to Israel, to her survival and welfare. It means support for the exodus of Soviet Jews and their settlement in Israel. It means responsibility for the rescue of the remaining Ethiopian Jews from Africa.

"Never again" means identifying with the Jewish community and participating in the joys and sorrows of our Jewish people. It means accepting the obligation of Torah study and the practice of Mitzvot so that the Jewish people may survive not only physically and biologically but also keep faith with its spiritual destiny.

Only then do we give meaning to the slogan "Never again."

At the exit from Yad Vashem in Jerusalem, before the visitor leaves, he reads a quotation ascribed to the founder of Chasidism: *"Forgetting prolongs the exile; remembering is the secret of redemption."*

If we forget, we shall continue to widen the gulf of alienation that separates us, God's children all, from one another and from God. If we remember, we may yet be able to pass from the shadow of the Holocaust and its impenetrable mysteries.

Through remembrance, we may yet emerge from the landscape of death, from the valley of tears, and turn the dawn of a new day into a future of hope and redemption.

1 *Toronto Star, December '89 AP Sunrise, Fla.*

Through Exile or Redemption?

"Apologia pro Vita Sua."

This is the phrase literary critics sometimes use to pigeonhole a work which they judge an author has written, intentionally or not, as self-vindication: "An apology for his life." Rabbis may sometimes preach sermons that are in essence apologetic: attempts to justify what they have done or failed to do. They may not always be aware of it.

I am open to the reproach -if such it is- that the sermon "Through Exile or Redemption?" belongs to this class. I may have preached it to rationalize to myself and to others why I have made my home in Canada and never made Aliya. To settle in Israel would have been logical in view of my Zionist belief. Moreover, my fate in Germany should have taught me once and for all that it is foolish for a Jew to seek full political, cultural and social integration in a nation not really his own; that only living in a Jewish country can we Jews find safety and self-respect. My subsequent experiences in England and my two years of internment in Canada should have convinced me of the absurdity for Jews to count on the good will of other people, be they ever so democratic and generally fair.

Yet I stayed in Canada and despite my initial disappointments I opted for being a Canadian and for meaningful participation in the life of my adopted country. Despite my Zionist ideology, I consider Jewish life in the Diaspora not a make-shift provisional arrangement, but a spiritually valid option as a mode of Jewish life.

Of course, I have had to wrestle with this question spiritually. This sermon is a product of my internal struggle. As a religious leader, I must know that other Jews have similar conflicts and are entitled to my guidance, or at least to an articulation of their problem. If it is necessary to write an "apologia" for my life, then the existence of our Canadian Jewish community and our efforts on its behalf also require a thoughtful rationale.

The germane question is whether this sermon represents an objective and truthful position or whether it is a shaky excuse after the fact.

I leave the answer to this question to my readers. I feel I have addressed the problem objectively and I believe that my conclusions are a valid interpretation of the Rabbinic passage I used as my text.

Through Exile or Redemption? ——————
A sermon preached on the Sabbath of Chanukah 5733 - 1972

> *Jacob settled in the land where his father had dwelled*
> *(Gen. 37:1).*

We could almost hear the sigh of relief in the verse with which the Torah reading began today.

Jacob had returned. He had survived his exile. He had escaped from danger. For the moment, at least, he was secure against envious enemies.

Home again! Safe at last!

His offspring was not so fortunate! When Jacob's descendants, after surviving their exile, returned to the newly created State of Israel, they had no such respite. There was not even time to draw a sigh of relief.

Terrorism, siege and aggression preceded, accompanied and followed the declaration of Israel's Independence in May 1948.

In spite of all this, the birth of the Jewish State instantly revolutionized the status of the Jewish people. It was a radical transformation. For the first time in more than two thousand years, the Jewish people controlled a piece of its homeland.

One of the first acts of Jewish sovereignty was the enactment of the Law of Return. Every Jew in the world was given the right to come back home to Israel as a citizen. The Law of Return facilitated an immediate and unprecedented ingathering of the exiles.

From that point on, a question mark has been hanging over the Jews of the dispersion, the "Diaspora," or "Golah" in classical Hebrew.

During the centuries of exile, return to Zion had been problematic, difficult or even impossible. In 1948, the gates were flung wide open. No Turk, no Briton, held the key; no White Paper could deny access any longer.

Exile, in Hebrew "Galut," the condition of living away from the Jewish land, was once forced on us by circumstances beyond our control. Now it became voluntary, a matter of personal choice.

Why indeed should we remain in exile?

Many of our neighbours look at us as intruders, as foreigners or as aliens to be tolerated, at best. The barbs and taunts of anti-Semitism are part of our normal experience.

Why be satisfied with living only partly Jewish lives; why compromise?

The language we speak is not a Jewish language. To observe the Shabbat is a handicap; to keep Kashrut is difficult and a barrier to "normal" life. Why should we put up with University exams scheduled for Passover or graduations on Friday night? Whatever success a Jew achieves, in business, in the academic world or in politics, benefits another country, not our own. The art we create is Canadian, not Jewish art; our writers enrich Canadian, not Jewish literature.

So, some of us go on Aliyah. They settle in Israel. They pack in the "Galut." They had enough of being strangers, outsiders and dichotomized people.

They return "home."

"If I become a farmer," says the "Oleh," the new immigrant in Israel, "I help build a Jewish country; if I am successful in business, I have the satisfaction of enriching a new Jewish economy. If my child becomes a famous scientist, he or she will bring benefit and renown to Israel. If he becomes a poet, he will be a Jewish poet. Meanwhile, he will learn the Bible in school and speak Hebrew on the street. I don't have to tremble when she starts dating. And above all, I don't depend on the toleration of the Gentiles."

Are we who have stayed in the diaspora really the cop-outs?

Do we lack the guts, the courage and the idealism to take the big, decisive step that being Jewish really mandates? Many Israelis look at us in this light.

176

Indeed, some of us do feel ill-at-ease or embarrassed at this weakness of our Jewish commitment. Admittedly, we compromise. We cite a multitude of reasons to stay where we are: economics, family ties, children and personal roots. We rationalize that there cannot be enough room in Israel for every Jew to return! Besides, do we not need UJA contributors and State of Israel Bond buyers to keep Israel going?

Are there better reasons to justify our remaining in the diaspora?

I would like to present my positive answer on the basis of the Haftara, the Reading from the Prophets, for the Shabbat of Chanukah. This selection from the Prophet Zechariah (3:14-4:7) contains his famous vision of the "Menorah," the candelabrum.

The original Menorah provided light in the Temple. In time, the Menorah became the favourite symbol representing the people of Israel. The modern State of Israel adopted the Menorah as its official emblem.

In Zechariah's vision, he saw a Menorah whose seven lamps were supplied with oil from a bowl. The Hebrew word for bowl is "Gulla." Oil flowed from two olive trees into the bowl, and seven miniature pipe lines carried it to the seven lamps of the Menorah.

A comment by our ancient Rabbis focuses on the word "Gulla", the bowl. The Rabbis note its similarity to two other Hebrew words.

One teacher holds that "Gulla" relates to "G'ulla", the Hebrew word for "Redemption, Ingathering." The other teacher derives it from "Gola", the word for "Diaspora or Dispersion."

It seems to me that these two teachers wish to present antithetical models of Jews and Judaism.

The first teacher sees the light of the Menorah originating from "G'ulla," redemption and sovereignty. Only Redemption can supply the oil for our lamp. Only a redeemed people of Israel, creating its own distinctive society, can be a light to the world.

The second teacher disagrees. The Menorah is nourished by the "Gola." The "Diaspora Jew" is not necessarily a pitiable compromise, but may represent an authentic alternative model of Jewish existence. Jews can and must fulfil their role as a light unto humanity even while living among the nations of the world.

It would be self-deception to attribute our reluctance to make Aliyah to high and noble motives. But, just as certainly, Judaism and the world would be poorer if there were no diaspora.

There are Jewish and human values which Jews can represent and illustrate only by living as a minority; similarly, there are other values which only a sovereign Jewish majority can actualize.

In a beautiful story told in the Midrash, the angels raise objections to God's plan to create human beings. Humans are weak and wicked, the angels claim, not worthy of being created.

God does not agree. "Do you know what evil is? Do you have an evil inclination?" he asks his angelic critics. "Do you understand what it means to be human, to have to work for a livelihood, to know evil, to be exposed to temptation and still to try to obey my command?"

There is a kind of grandeur in Jewish life in the diaspora.

It is glorious and heroic to live in a free Jewish country. But there is also a unique opportunity for "Kiddush Hashem," for the sanctification of God, in the challenge to remain Jewish under the pressures of living in the dispersion. There is a great deal of valour and courage demanded of those who follow the Jewish way of life while exposed to the lures of a non-Jewish world and the temptation to blend in with a secular majority culture.

Eastern Europe was filled with Jewish communities, large and small, in which Jews created a beautiful and unique model of Jewish life. In hostile surroundings, they achieved spiritual heights of a kind and a degree that an emancipated or a sovereign Jewish society has not yet been able to produce and, by virtue of its very nature, cannot ever produce.

The Chasid, who lit a flame of piety and joy in the darkest depth of exile, was a unique and authentic Jewish phenomenon. He and the values incarnate in him deserve perpetuation, not merely a place in history.

The Diaspora Jew whose career choice is determined by his desire to keep Shabbat, at the sacrifice perhaps of some personal inclinations and talents, represents a type of piety that is of permanent value.

The isolated small-town Jewish family which maintains Kashrut, practices hospitality and brings respect to the name "Jew" in a forsaken corner of the world, fulfils an important part of the Jewish purpose.

A Jew who enters public life and contributes to the welfare of his adopted or native land is an authentic model of being Jewish.

Building Synagogues and other community institutions, without state financing but entirely by voluntary contributions, is a unique virtue of the American diaspora and a glorious chapter in our history.

Living in two worlds, as many of us do, is not just a compromise. It is exciting. It is exciting to experience the dynamics of influences flowing back and forth between our Jewish world and our wider social context. These influences are mutually beneficial and enriching.

Combining a Jewish life with full participation in the general society is not necessarily an expedient ad hoc arrangement. It qualifies as a legitimate form of Judaism. Developed in the distress, the trials and errors, the hopes and the frustrations of two thousand years, this model of Judaism was not meant to be liquidated as obsolete after the creation of the State of Israel. Co-existence is legitimate. "Gola" and "G'ulla" are two valid manifestations of one Judaism.

Before Israel came into being, the exile was dark and unbearable. Now Israel exists. The Menorah of the Jewish people will shine forth. The redeemed Jewish society in Israel and viable Jewish communities scattered in the diaspora will share in supplying the fuel for its flame.

A Martyr on the Beach

In the summer of 1990, a tragedy shook the Toronto community, Adath Israel in particular. An explosive device planted on a crowded beach in Tel Aviv killed Marnie Kimelman, a young Torontonian visiting Israel. Marnie was on an Israel summer program with hundreds of other youngsters under the auspices and leadership of the Canadian Zionist Federation. No one else was killed or seriously injured in the blast.

Marnie was a brilliant, idealistic, and popular young lady, deeply committed to Judaism and the State of Israel. She was a leader among her peers. Her tragic death, therefore, brought deep anguish and despair, not only to her family but also to the other participants in the program, to her fellow students and numerous friends.

When schools were about to reopen after the summer vacation, a Memorial Service, in tribute to Marnie, was held. It was hoped that the Service might help especially the young mourners to recover from the emotional and spiritual shock of tragic bereavement. The Service, under the auspices of the Canadian Zionist Federation of Canada, took place at her family's Congregation, the Adath Israel Synagogue. I was asked to be the principal speaker.

In the course of my Rabbinic office, I was called many times to articulate a response to tragedy. However, for the tragic dimensions of Marnie's death I had no parallels in my previous experience. In the presence of her family and friends, and a large number of compassionate and concerned members of the community, I approached my assignment with a feeling of helplessness and great trepidation.

A Martyr on the Beach ─────────────
An Address at a Memorial Service for Marnie Kimelman
September 5, 1990

The Torah reading on the morning of Yom Kippur contains the order of the Biblical ritual on the Day of Atonement. Curiously, the chapter begins with a reference to the death of Aaron's sons.

> *The Lord spoke to Moses after the death of the two sons*
> *of Aaron who died when they drew near to the Lord.*

> (Leviticus 16:1)

Why are the instructions for the Day of Atonement introduced by this reference to Aaron's tragedy? What is the connection between the death of his sons and this Holy Day?

The answer given by our ancient sages is deeply meaningful:

ללמדך שכשם שיום הכפורים מכפר על ישראל
כן מיתתן של צדיקים מכפרת על ישראל.

> *The mention of the death of Aaron's sons comes to teach*
> *you that just as Yom Kippur brings atonement to the*
> *people of Israel, thus the death of the righteous brings*
> *atonement to the people of Israel.*

> (Jerusalem Talmud Yoma 1:1)

The human mind wrestles with the perennial problem of evil.

Why does evil exist?

Why do bad things befall innocent people?

Among the many disturbing questions triggered by undeserved suffering and inexplicable evil, there is an especially agonizing mystery: the death of the young.

Why should it ever happen? And how could it happen, in the case of Aaron's sons, *"when they drew near to God?"* At this moment of sacred service, engaged in the task of ministering in the Tabernacle on the day of its consecration, they ought to have been immune from any kind of mishap or calamity!

What, then, are we to say about Marnie, an idealistic girl, motivated to visit Israel by her devotion and love for the country, only to die in an outrageous terrorist act?

181

Did she travel thousands of miles to keep an appointment with her destiny?

So unique are the circumstances of her death, that we cannot possibly call it an "accident."

The word "accident" is derived from the Latin. It means something that falls on us in a random fashion.

Marnie's death was too singular, too unique; it was as if it had been foreordained, as if Providence had singled her out with a purpose!

It was not as if she had happened to travel to a place where an earthquake suddenly struck and claimed thousands of victims; as if she had been one among many passengers killed in a plane crash. No, she was the only victim of a terrorist bomb meant for anyone, not for her in particular.

There were thousands of people on the beach in Tel Aviv at that time. Against all statistical odds, Marnie was selected in the macabre lottery of death.

She was one of us. Our own community was struck. A family in our own midst was burdened with tragic sorrow.

They were our own kids who while on a fun-filled summer experience in Israel lost the insulating innocence that shields the young from the knowledge of death and grief and accident and tragedy. Our own children had to face their unexpected vulnerability.

It is for this reason that we are here. We must try to come to terms with our own tragedy.

We owe Marnie, her friends, her companions and ourselves, a response to her death.

We must seize the tangled threads of our poor, deficient understanding and weave them into a design of meaning.

There is a difference between giving an explanation and finding a meaning. We are unable to produce a rationale, but we can search for meaning.

We must try to express what Marnie's precious life and untimely death may mean for us, and thus we may try to mend the heartbreak of her peers and friends. Though she died tragically, senselessly, and though nothing can palliate the hurt of her loved ones, at least we may know she did not die in vain.

182

I would like to take recourse, therefore, in the Rabbinic proposition that there was meaning in the death of Aaron's children:

"The death of the righteous is an atonement for Israel."

Marnie's martyrdom must have a redemptive effect on us. Its effect on us must be one of cleansing, of purifying, similar to the experience of Yom Kippur. Life itself must become more precious, more sacred, and be raised to a higher dimension.

Marnie's death must make us all better human beings.

It must be our incentive to renew our idealistic commitments.

Marnie was known as the "peace lady" because of her love of peace and her skill at mediating quarrels or arguments. We must therefore strengthen our own commitment to the pursuit of peace and the avoidance of contention.

We must consider always the destructive, corrosive effect of hatred, an emotion to which Marnie was a complete stranger. We must remember that it was hatred that took her away from us!

What a horrible thought: somewhere a human being rejoiced that a bomb he planted killed someone!

We must never rejoice at the death of an enemy, remembering that every act of killing is fratricide, for all human beings are brothers and sisters.

Marnie would tell us that hatred corrupts us. Marnie would have us commit ourselves diligently to the improvement of our world by non-violent means, and strive for justice and peace.

Moses tried to comfort Aaron with the thought that God is hallowed by those dearest to him. The commentator Rashi elaborates Moses' words:

אהרן אחי, יודע הייתי שיתקדש הבית במיודעיו
של מקום. והייתי סבור או בי או בך,
עכשיו רואה אני שהם גדולים ממני וממך.

Aaron, my brother, I knew that the sanctuary had to be hallowed by God's intimates; so I thought either by you or by me. Now I realize that they were closer to God than either of us. (Leviticus 10:3)

In His mysterious ways, God chose Marnie to hallow our love for Israel.

She loved the country and she loved the last weeks of her young life in Israel. Her death was for Israel; she was killed because she represented Israel. Her death must hallow our love, making it stronger and invulnerable.

Terrorism is intended to induce fear, to intimidate, to deter us from following our convictions. However, it achieves the opposite because we shall always feel even more strongly Marnie's love for the Jewish people, the Jewish homeland and the people of Israel.

Marnie's sacrifice commits us to work for an Israel free from threats, secure and accepted, and capable of carrying out its destined role to be the instrument of redemption for the Jewish people and a light unto the world.

In that light of redemption, of universal love and global peace, there will shine for all time the memory of those who sacrificed their lives for Israel, and that sacred company includes Marnie Kimelman. May her memory be a blessing!

Rebuilding the Temple

Rabbinic statements recorded in the Talmud show that some of the Sages, notwithstanding their fervent hope for the coming of the Messiah, did not want to live through the anticipated period of upheaval and cataclysm preceding his advent.

There is no way of comparing the events of the twentieth century with the frightened expectations of the ancient Rabbis. No doubt many of those who lived through the catastrophies of this century would have preferred to be born into a more tranquil age. I, however, feel that despite the agony, the horror and the grief, it was a privilege to experience the ordeals of our era. The wrenching intensity of life in our time and of witnessing revolutionary changes at an incredibly rapid pace, could not have been experienced in any other period of history. To have passed through the vicissitudes of our era and to have emerged alive means to have been one of destiny's favourites.

A neighbouring congregation, Beth David Bnai Israel Beth Am, invited me to be the guest preacher on the Sabbath commemorating the 36th anniversary of the congregation. The invitation had very personal overtones. I had been a life-long friend of Rabbi Albert Pappenheim, the beloved founding Rabbi of the Congregation. The congregational anniversary was unthinkable without a meaningful reference to his ministry that ended with his premature death in 1984. [1]

The fabric of my sermon was woven therefore around the historical experiences and personal destiny which Rabbi Pappenheim and I had shared: the destruction of the German-Jewish community and the phenomenal growth of a mature Jewish community in Toronto and generally on the North American continent.

Rebuilding the Temple

A Sermon preached at the Beth David Bnai Israel Beth Am Congregation, Toronto, on Parshat Vayeira - November 3, 1990

The warmth of Rabbi Scheim's [2] gracious introduction reflects feelings that are mutual. My relationship with your congregation was created by my friendship with the late Rabbi Albert Pappenheim. It has been reinforced by my admiration for Rabbi Scheim whose dedication, maturity, courage and determination have provided leadership and continuity.

Rabbi Pappenheim's Hebrew name was *"Avraham,"* our ancestor who by a meaningful co-incidence is the hero of today's Torah portion. I would like to refer to a salient point in it.

Abraham has passed the supreme test. He has proved his absolute submission to God and offered a ram on the altar on which he had been ready to sacrifice his son Isaac.

Now, Abraham is about to give a name to the place of his sacrifice. It is a prophetic moment; for he will be naming the site of the future temple.

> *Abraham named that site "Hashem yir'eh - the Lord sees," whence the present saying, "On the mountain of the Lord there is vision."* (Genesis 22:14)

The meaning of the passage is a little mystifying. The Sages cut through the obscurity of the Hebrew text with an imaginative comment: *"The verse teaches that God showed Abraham the Temple built, destroyed and rebuilt"* (Sifri Devarim 352).

Abraham saw the Temple in Jerusalem in three stages: in its original splendour, then as a heap of ruins on a scorched mountain top and finally, restored to its sacred beauty and glory.

Is there a difference between the first stage and the third? Certainly. The restored temple will lack the triumphant innocence of the pristine original. It may look the same, but behind the restored facade there hides the haunting memory of destruction.

The shape of the rebuilt temple has matured through suffering. The wood has been seasoned by the knowledge of ruin. The stones vibrate with the echoes of the yearning of generations.

186

With us today are many who have been witnesses of the upheavals of the twentieth century. They have seen this triple vision of building, destruction and rebuilding.

Certainly the Abraham who helped to build this Synagogue saw this triple vision.

In our youth, which Rabbi Pappenhein and I shared, we saw a Jewish world built by the cumulative labour of many generations.We remember the heartland of European Jewry, a magnificent temple of Torah, piety and Jewish learning.

Then came destruction. This week we shall observe the anniversary of Crystal Night, the night of violence and fire which foreshadowed the ruin of European Jewry, the Holocaust which turned Jewish communities into smouldering heaps of ashes.

And then we witnessed the miraculous rebuilding. We saw the rise of the State of Israel. We experienced the amazing transfer of Jewish vitality and leadership to the American continent.

Your Congregation and your Rabbi were part of this process.

That is what we celebrate today. It is not just the anniversary of a Synagogue, but of your Synagogue as the paradigm of re-creating, of restoration and of redemption.

Beth David, the beautiful name of your Congregation, recalls our ancient King.

An interesting Talmudic story (Brachot 3b) tells us how King David's harp would hang over his bed when he went to sleep. At midnight, the north wind, the *"Ruach [3] Tzefonit,"* would blow over the strings, and the harp *"m'naggen mei-alav - would play by itself."* At once, King David would rise and engage in the study of Torah.

A peculiar story, isn't it? Did King David have an early model of the musical alarm clock? Why was it the north wind in particular that activated the harp and deprived the King of his sleep?

The key to the meaning of the story may be found in the Talmudic passage (Baba Batra 28b) that contains the following counsel.

> He who wants to become wise, let him turn south; he
> who wants to become rich, turn north.

187

The south of the Land of Israel, the Negev, was once famous for its wise men, while the fertile valleys of the north held a promise of wealth.

Now we understand. When the *"Ruach"* of the north - the spirit of affluence - blows, *"the harp plays by itself."* Wealthy patrons will build concert halls, endow orchestras, and provide funding for the theatre. There will be little need to worry about the arts.

It is about Torah that we must worry.

Torah requires effort and sacrifice. Study and observance, devotion and spirituality demand personal commitment and a great measure of renunciation. Especially when the north wind blows, when the music of the harp sounds so beautiful and enticing, David must arise, give up his comforts and begin his lonely vigil studying the Torah.

When Rabbi Pappenheim and I were fellow students at a Yeshiva in London, England, we witnessed an episode that I never forgot.

The entire student body of the Yeshiva consisted of young refugees from Germany, Austria, Czechoslovakia and Hungary. Many of the students knew no English and were anxious to remedy this deficiency, a handicap in an English-speaking country. One day a student delegation approached the head of the Yeshiva, Rabbi Moshe Schneider, with the request that the Yeshiva institute English classes.

The Rabbi was aghast. He asked us to step over to the window: "Look outside!" he said. "Do you see all the people in the street? They all speak English: the taxi driver, the mother wheeling the pram, even the garbage man heaving the bins into his truck. Do you think God saved you from Hitler's clutches because he needed more English speakers in London? There is no shortage of English here! There is a shortage of Torah! For that you are needed here. That is the purpose for which God saved you and brought you to this country!"

The memory of this scene has always been a great help to me. It helps me rationalize our separate existence as Jews. Why must we Jews survive? Our raison d'être lies not in the similarities we share with others, but in our differences, in our distinctiveness and uniqueness.

It is fair, of course, to point also to common elements which we share with our non-Jewish fellow citizens. There are many of those. They facilitate our integration into the wider community. However, our real value lies in what is uniquely Jewish. If the world needs Jews, and if God wants Jews, it is not for what other people can do equally well, but for values that are peculiar to us.

The health of our ecological environment, social justice, world peace — all these and others are important issues and part of our Jewish commitment. However, they are not our exclusive responsibility; others are just as responsible and capable as we to address these issues.

Torah - that is our specialty! No one else can take our place.

By Torah I mean genuine, authentic Judaism, characterized by knowledge, by faithfulness to Mitzvot, spirituality, adherence to a Jewish way of life and by the passionate pursuit of Jewish goals.

Our Synagogues stand for an enlightened commitment to Torah in this broad sense. Through the celebration of your Synagogue's Anniversary, you confirm this commitment.

Rabbi Pappenheim would have called it "Torah im Derech Eretz," [4] a classic phrase used by German Jews to describe a distinct philosophy that advocated a synthesis of Torah and general culture.

I call it an enlightened commitment to Torah because it does not require us to wear intellectual blinkers.

Our commitment calls for Torah as the organizing principle of all our values: our participation in our country, our devotion to Zion, to peace and to justice and our determination to create a healthy physical and moral environment for ourselves and generations to come.

Let the generation that remembers the old world in its glory, the generation that witnessed its destruction and disappearance, help the new generation to build the new temple. Together, let us create a new community *"b'har hashem yeira'eh"* [5] - on the lofty mountain top that affords us a vision of God, of the earth as His Kingdom, of our Synagogues as the network of His spirit and of our hearts and homes as His abode!

[1] *See "Jethro: A Memorial Tribute to Rabbi Albert Pappenheim" on page 64*

[2] *Rabbi Philip Scheim, Assistant Rabbi at the time of Rabbi Pappenheim's death, was appointed to succeed him.*

[3] *The Hebrew word "ruach" denotes "spirit" as well as "wind."*

[4] *literally: "Torah with a worldly way" - an expression used in the Talmud for a combination of Torah study with a secular occupation*

[5] *Genesis 22:14, cited above, "on the mountain of the Lord there is vision."*

Life is a Four-Letter Word

What came first: the chicken or the egg?

What was created first: heaven or earth? The academies of Hillel and Shammai held opposite views on the order of creation (Talmud Hagiga 12a), while other Sages asserted that heaven and earth were created together as one.

A similar enigma shrouds the genesis of a sermon: "Do you first select the subject or the text?"

There is no firm rule for me, I answer. Often the topic comes first. At other times, a text is so irresistible and overwhelming that the sermon will develop simply and almost spontaneously from the text.

Very often, theme and text, like heaven and earth, materialize together.

I came across a string of four Midrashim on the secret of life. The initials of the key words form the acronym "Chayim," the Hebrew word for Life. I could not resist preaching this text. I was also tempted to spin my own Midrash by treating the English word "Life" as an acronym. I yielded to the temptation.

Although in this case the text preceded the theme, I would not have found the text so compelling if it had not been so contrary to most modern prescriptions for a good life quality.

Many modern people cling to a very sanitized view of life. They believe, for example, that pain is not normal but due to some mistake, hopefully avoidable. In love with independence, they reject the idea that the will of anyone else ought to control our lives. Fear is to be outgrown. Pleasure, not wisdom, is the ultimate objective. Against this shallow perspective, the Midrash posits a less popular, but more deeply Jewish concept of the good life.

My own Midrash, I hope, adds a contemporary dimension to the quest for meaning in our lives.

191

Life is a Four-Letter Word _____
A Sermon preached on Yom Kippur 5750 - 1989

What is on top of our Yom Kippur wish-list? What do we want most?

Life!

> *Zochreinu l'chayim - O remember us for Life!*
> *Kotveinu b'sefer hachayim - inscribe us in the Book of Life!* (Mahzor)

Life is what it's all about.

A four-letter word.

We want a good life, of course; a quality life. If possible, we want to enjoy health, wealth and "nachas," but we want life in any case, for as Scripture puts it, *"better to be a living dog than a dead lion"* (Ecclesiastes 9:4).

But is mere life, bare survival, enough? Certainly not.

We want to get something out of life. We want life to have purpose and meaning. We want our life to make sense.

A meaningful life cannot be one of isolation. It must be connected with the lives of others. In this hour of Yizkor, we feel the need of connecting our lives with the lives of our departed. We want their lives to be joined to ours *"bitzror hachayim - in the bond of the living."*

To give meaning to our lives is the hope of Yom Kippur.

תודיעני אורח חיים

"teach me the path of life!" (Psalm 16:11).

Don't give me life simply as a gift, but teach me how to create it. Show me the way on which I must proceed in order to experience life, the meaningful, purposeful, sense-making life!

Teach me what I must put into it and what I may expect to get out of it!

The Sages want to show us the path of life in four Midrashim on the Biblical book of Proverbs. Each Midrash comments on one of four references to life found in different passages in the Biblical Book of Proverbs. Each Midrash starts with the prayer for the path of life found in Psalm 16, a prayer presumably uttered by King David, the traditional author of the Psalms.

"Teach me the path to life," David asked God.

Said God to David:

אם חיים אתה מבקש צפה לחכמה

"If you want Life, seek Wisdom, for so it is written

עץ חיים היא למחזיקים בה

' — it (i.e. Wisdom) is a tree of life to those who grasp it' (Proverbs 3:18);

אם חיים אתה מבקש צפה ליראה

if you want Life, seek the Fear of God, for so it is written'

יראת ה' תוסיף חיים

' — the Fear of the Lord prolongs life' (Proverbs 10:27);

אם חיים אתה מבקש צפה ליסורין

if you want Life, seek Pain, for so it is written '

ודרך היים תוכחות מוסר

' — the way to life is rebuke through painful discipline' (Proverbs 6:23);

אם חיים אתה מבקש צפה למצוות

if you want Life, seek Mitzvot, the Commandments, for so it is written '

שמור מצוותי וחיה

— keep my commandments and live!'"
(Proverbs 4:4 and 7:2).

Here then is our Sages' prescription for Life: *Chochma - Wisdom; Yir'a - Fear of God; Yissurin - Pain;* and *Mitzvot - Commandments.*

Take the initials of these four words, *chochma, yir'a, yissurin, mitzvot: chet, yud, yud, mem.* What do they spell?

"Chayyim - Life!"

"Chayim" is the acronym of Wisdom, Fear of God, Pain, and Commandments!

Many people believe that three P's are the keys to Life: profit, pleasure, power. But profit cannot buy happiness; pleasure becomes stale and makes insatiable demands; and power corrupts. The three P's do not point to the path of life.

No. If you want Life, you need Wisdom. Live intelligently. Strive for knowledge. Explore the wonders of nature and the miracle of the human being. Know yourself, and try to understand our world and our history. Study Torah and seek Jewish knowledge, for the Wisdom of Torah will enrich your life and add to it a new dimension of meaning.

If you want Life, you need the Fear of God. We human beings are apt to stray. Laws can be circumvented. People can be fooled. Our principles can be bent. Only the fear of God will keep us on the straight and narrow. If we believe God is our all-seeing, all-knowing Judge, that belief will help us to remain honest and good. It will give us the strength, when needed, to withstand peer pressure and will harden our rock-bottom resistance, if our superiors will ever try to coerce us to carry out immoral orders.

If you want Life, you also need a dose of suffering. You need pain. Strange, isn't it, how people believe that to suffer pain or discomfort is abnormal. A normal life, they think, is constantly pleasurable. At the least twinge of an ache or other discomfort, some people will head straight for the medicine cabinet. A few of us carry around a veritable pharmacy for any contingency! Of course, serious pain should be attended to, but a little bit of occasional pain is good for you. It is part of life. Life abounds with unavoidable suffering: conflict, loss, disappointment, defeat, depression, sadness and anguish. Don't run away from these experiences! They belong to life just as much as happiness, victories and rewards. Our experiences of pain are often closer to the truth of life. And pain ennobles. It may teach you new insights and make you a better person with heightened sensitivity and empathy.

Last, but not least, if you want Life, carry out God's commandments. Do His will; don't run after foolish whims and multitudinous, ever-changing desires, but carry out God's mandates. Be His agent in this world. In doing so, you will come closer to human perfection, closer to God from whom your human dignity derives. You will make your life a Jewish life and become attached to the eternal Jewish people. You will make the world a better place, a clearer reflection of the Divine design. Remember, it is impossible to be a good Jew or a good person "in your heart" only. You must actualize what is inside you through deeds, through action, through Mitzvot. They enhance our lives and augment the spirituality of the world.

Thus, according to our ancient Sages, Wisdom, Fear of God, Pain, and Mitzvot add up to "Chayim," a meaningful life.

After 2000 years, their comment is still valid and relevant. But we need not stop here. Just as they expounded "Chayim" as an acronym, let us interpret the four-letter word "Life" in a similar fashion.

The "L" stands for Love. If you want to experience life fully, you must love. With the dawn of your own self-awareness, you learn to love parents. As you grow, you learn to love others: siblings, friends, grandparents. You experience the revelation of romantic love. You love a spouse; you love your children and eventually grandchildren. How poor life would be without these experiences! How we would restrict life's scope, if we were to suppress love!

The growth of love does not stop with the love of individuals. We must develop a loving attitude. We must open our hearts to people and to the world. We must be willing to feel, to have emotions. Important though wisdom is, our lives would be cold and sterile without emotions. Yet the emotional life is risky: you may get hurt. It has been said: *"Life is a comedy for those who think, and a tragedy for those who feel."* A poetic exaggeration, perhaps, but it is true, no doubt, that a willingness to love makes you vulnerable. All the same, if you want to live, love!

The "I" means Involvement. If you remain an island, life will pass you by. Commit yourself! Be involved! Put your whole self where your heart is! Become important to a good cause! Care for your community, for your people, for the environment!. Don't live selfishly! *"If I am for myself only, what am I?"* the great Sage Hillel said (Pirke Avot 1:14). When you are needed by friends, by neighbours, by your children's school, by your Synagogue, do you say "I have my own troubles. What do I need this for?" If that is your attitude, you may miss some of life's greatest adventures and deepest satisfactions.

The "F" must stand for Faith. If you lack faith, your life is without an anchor. You are not firmly established. The Hebrew word for Faith is *"Emunah,"* from a root meaning "to be firm." Faith in God gives you confidence. Faith in values gives you direction. Faith in life's ultimate goodness gives you optimism and hope. A measure of skepticism may be healthy. We should not accept everything at face value. But without faith we are deficient. We cannot reach our full potential. There are summits to which only faith can lift us.

"E." What should the final letter of "Life" stand for? For me, "E" means Ecstacy. Ecstacy is a form of joy. The Greek word from which "ecstacy" is derived means "to be outside of one's state of equilibrium." To be ecstatic means to abandon our normalcy, to allow ourselves to lose our balance and to let rapture possess us.

Whether admiring a sunset or surrendering to the magic of music or art, the capacity to become excited by the enjoyment of beauty is one example of ecstacy. To enjoy friendship or love without selfish motive is another. To rejoice when good fortune comes our way, or to share the joy of others, is also a form of being "outside of ourselves," and so is the capacity of "letting our hair down" on occasion. Life cannot always be serious. There has to be laughter, humour, joy, even foolishness. Ecstacy stands for the ability to celebrate life, to say "yes" to it, to want it and to love it.

"Teach me the path of life!" In Hebrew and in English, may the four letters of life instruct us in the art of living!

The
GLOSSARY

ADAR
> A month in the Jewish calendar occurring in late winter to early spring.

ADATH ISRAEL
> The name of the Congregation as whose Rabbi the author served from 1947 to 1989. The name means "Congregation of Israel."

ADON OLAM
> A hymn chanted at the end of the service in many congregations.

AGGADA
> Literally "the telling." Aggada is the non-legal part of Rabbinic literature: stories, folklore, philosophy, etc. See "What a Difference a Psalm Makes!" It is the antonym of "Halacha" (see Glossary).

AKEDA
> "The Binding"; refers to the binding of Isaac on the altar. The word epitomizes Abraham's complete submission to God, even at the sacrifice of his own son Isaac.

ALIYA (pl. Aliyot)
> The "going up." 1. Going up to the Reading of the Torah at public worship. The Torah portion is read to several individuals who take their position in sequence beside the Reader and recite a blessing before and after a section is read for them. To be called to the Torah Reading is to have an "Aliya." 2. Going up to the Holy Land to settle there is called "Aliya."

AMIDAH
> The "Standing Prayer," a major component of the liturgy of every prayer service.

BAR MITZVAH
> Technically, a designation of a person obligated to fulfil the Commandment (see "Mitzva, Mitzvot"). It is commonly used to describe the celebration of coming of age in the religious sense and of assuming the responsibilities of Jewish adulthood. Boys become Bar Mitzvah at age thirteen, girls Bat Mitzvah at twelve.

BEN GURION, DAVID
> The first Prime Minister of Israel; was Prime Minister 1949-1952 and 1954-1965.

199

BUBBE, BUBBIE
Yiddish for "grandmother." A **"Bubbe Maisse"** is an "old-wives tale."

CHANUKA
"Dedication"; the Festival instituted to celebrate annually the rededication of the Temple in Jerusalem after the successful Maccabean revolt against the Hellenistic Empire (ca. 165 B.C.E.). Also called the "Festival of Lights" after the ceremony of lighting candles or oil lamps every night of the eight-day festival.

CHASID, (Pl. Chasidim)
An adherent of "Chasidism," a popular religious movement originating in Eastern Europe in the 17th Century. Chasidism was characterized by its emphasis on emotion, particularly on joy, in the performance of the Mitzvot (see Glossary), by mysticism and by the centrality of the "Rebbe," the charismatic Rabbinic leader of each of the many diverse Chasidic communities.

CHASIDIC:
pertaining to, or characteristic of, Chasidism.

CHAVER (Pl. Chaverim)
friend, companion, fellow, member, associate.

CHAVRUSA
Literally "society, companionship," term used in the Yeshiva (see Glossary) for a study partner.

CHAZAN, CHAZANIM; CHAZANUT
Chazanut is the musical art of the Synagogue. "Chazan" is the Cantor, plural "Chazanim."

CONSERVATIVE JUDAISM
A modern, liberal yet traditional interpretation of Judaism that aims to synthesize tradition and change.

DREYFUS, ALFRED
Alfred Dreyfus, a Jewish captain in the French army, was the victim of an anti-Semitic conspiracy and convicted of espionage on October 15, 1894. His court-martial and conviction set off a wave of popular anti-Semitism in France. The Dreyfuss Affair also triggered vehement protests by Emile Zola and other writers, as a result of which his conviction was eventually overturned. The victim was returned from Devil's Island and rehabilitated in 1906.

GAN EDEN
> The Biblical Garden of Eden; paradise; the state or place of bliss after death.

GEHINNON
> Originally the name of a valley surrounding Jerusalem, it came to denote the state and place of punishment after death, roughly equivalent to Purgatory or Hell.

HAFTARA
> The "Conclusion"; a prescribed selection from the Prophetic Books which follows the Reading of the Torah on Shabbat and Festivals.

HAGGADA
> The book containing the liturgy for the "Seder," the "Order," the celebration of the Passover eve. The root of the word means "to tell," referring to the duty of telling the story of the Exodus.

HALACHA
> "The way to go"; the rules of Jewish law and the system, the processes and the literature of Jewish jurisprudence. Halacha facilitates and modifies the application of the "Mitzvot" (see Glossary) to life. See also "Aggada" and Introduction to "What a Difference a Psalm Makes!"

HAVDALA
> Literally "Separation"; a ceremony involving wine, spices and a light to mark the conclusion of the Shabbat and the beginning of the working week.

HAZANUT, HAZAN,
> See "Chazanut, Chazan"

HESCHEL, Prof. ABRAHAM JOSHUA (1907-1972)
> Scion of a renowned Chasidic family and an influential teacher at the Jewish Theological Seminary, New York. Rabbi Dr. Heschel was a profound thinker, philosopher, theologian and poet.

HIGH HOLIDAYS
> A popular way of referring to Rosh Hashana (see Glossary) and Yom Kippur (see Glossary.) The traditional Hebrew designation is "Yamim Nora'im - Days of Awe."

IYAR
> The name of a month in the Jewish calendar; occurs in the spring after Nissan, the month of Passover.

JUBILEE
>The Year of Release, the 50th year of the Jubilee cycle. The word is an English adaptation of the Hebrew "yovel," the "horn" whose sound announced the advent of the Year of Release for slaves and the restoration of sold ancestral lands.

KADDISH
>A frequently recurring doxology in the liturgy, extolling God's greatness and holiness and mentioning basic principles of faith, such as creation, providence and redemption. The "Kaddish" is also recited by mourners during their period of mourning when in attendance at public worship.

KASHRUT
>The body of rules applying to dietary prescriptions; or the state of being "kosher." See also "Kosher."

KIDDUSH
>"Sanctification"; a liturgical ceremony involving wine and bread at the beginning of the Shabbat and of Festivals. Also applied to the collation customarily following the morning services on Shabbat and Festivals.

KNESSET
>"Assembly" - The Israeli Parliament.

KOL NIDRE
>Literally "All Vows," the opening words of the liturgy for the eve of Yom Kippur. This section of the service, solemnly recited, is associated with the awe permeating the Day of Atonement, and supplies the name by which the evening and its religious service is known.

KOSHER
>Literally "prepared"; proper, usable, describing food allowed for eating. The opposite is "trefa," i.e. forbidden food, literally "torn" by a wild animal.

LEVITE
>Member of the Biblical tribe of Levi. Levites were functionaries of the Temple service, auxiliary to the Priests ("Kohanim") and supported by contributions from the Israelites.

MAROR
>The "Bitter Vegetables," eaten during the Passover ritual.

MATZA
>The Unleavened Bread of the Passover ritual.

MAHZOR

Literally "Cycle." The Mahzor is the Festival Prayer-book, the name reflecting the cyclical nature of the Festival calendar and its liturgy.

MAIMONIDES (1135-1204)

Rabbi Moses ben Maimon, the outstanding Jewish philosopher, theologian, jurist and savant of the Middle Ages. Of Spanish origin, he lived in Egypt where he was the chief physician of the Sultan.

MASHIACH - see Messiah

MASORTI

Hebrew for "Traditional," the name of Conservative Judaism in Israel.

MECHITZA

The physical partition separating women from men in the Synagogue.

MESSIAH

Anglicized version of Hebrew "Mashiah - the Anointed One," i.e. the King. A royal figure from the dynasty of David who will be the Redeemer to re-establish the Jewish Kingdom, gather in the exiles and usher in the Messianic era of peace.

MIDRASH

The word, from the root "DaRaSH - to seek, search" refers to a Rabbinic method of exegesis, of expounding the text of Scripture. Midrash searches for a deeper meaning, below the surface of the literal, by juxtaposing and comparing various text passages. The Midrashic method employs allegories, anecdotal history, numerology and various other expository devices. "The Midrash" may be used as a generic term to refer to the total literary record of this method. "A Midrash" (plural: "Midrashim") refers to a single Midrashic exposition of one passage. "Midrash" serves also to denote various collections of Midrashim on Biblical books; e.g. "Midrash Rabba," the "Great Midrash," etc.

MINHAG (pl. Minhagim)

A religious custom, often local and not required by law.

MINYAN

The "Count"; quorum of ten adult males required for public worship. A Minyan (plural Minyanim) is also a group of people who gather for worship.

MISHNA

From a root meaning "to repeat, rehearse, study," it refers to the early Rabbinic compilation of the Oral Law, the complement and supplement of the written Torah. It forms the basis of the Talmud.

MITZVA (Pl. Mitzvot)

"Commandment." The Mitzvot are the rules governing action and behaviour; the do's and don'ts, identified in the Torah by the rabbis. Following the system of Mitzvot enables the human being to govern his life by God's will. The word "Mitzvah" may also be used, somewhat loosely, in the meaning of "a good deed."

NACHAS

A Hebrew and Yiddish word, meaning "gratification, joy, satisfaction," used especially in Jewish parlance for the joyful rewards received from children or one's work.

NEILAH

The Closing Prayer; a service unique to Yom Kippur in the late afternoon.

NESHAMA

Hebrew for "Soul," derived from a root denoting breathing. See "Liberate Your Soul!"

NISSAN

The first month in the Biblical calendar, the month of Spring and Passover. See "A Tale of Two Walls."

ORTHODOXY, ORTHODOX JUDAISM

Designates in modern usage the non-liberal interpretation of Judaism and its adherents. It is characterized by strict interpretation of Jewish Law, by a conservative theology and resistance to the introduction of innovation.

PARSHAT - see TORAH PORTION

PASSOVER

Hebrew "Pesach"; the spring festival commemorating the exodus from Egypt.

PESACH

Hebrew for Passover

PURIM

A joyous festival commemorating the deliverance of the Jews of Persia from Haman's plot of genocide, described in the Biblical Book of "Esther." The word means "lots."

RABBI

An ordained teacher and interpreter of Jewish law and beliefs. "The Rabbis" often designates the classical teachers and interpreters of Judaism whose teachings are recorded in Talmud and Midrash.

RASHBAM

Acronym for Rabbi Samuel ben Meir (ca. 1080 - 1158), grandson of Rashi (see next entry); important exegete and Talmudist, France.

RASHI

The acronym by which one of the outstanding commentators on Torah and Talmud is known: Rabbi Shlomo ben Yitzchak (1040-1105), Germany and France.

RECONSTRUCTIONISM

A modern movement in Judaism founded by Prof. Mordechai Kaplan, of the Jewish Theological Seminary. Emphasizing that Judaism is an "evolving religious civilization" based on the peoplehood of Israel, it rejects supernaturalist and mystical elements in Judaism.

REFORM JUDAISM

A liberal interpretation of Judaism, originating in the nineteenth century period of Enlightenment, it rejects the traditional acceptance of Jewish law as obligatory and embraces insights of modernity.

ROSH HASHANA

"New Year"; the solemn festival beginning the "High Holy Days" period. Observed for two days, it is a time associated in Jewish tradition with an annual divine judgement, calling for introspection, self-scrutiny and repentance.

SHABBAT

"Sabbath," the weekly day of rest on the seventh day, i.e. Saturday.

SHECHUNA, SHECHINA

Two words derived from the same root which means "to reside, dwell." Shechuna is a settlement, a neighbourhood. Shechina is God's "in-dwelling," His Presence or Immanence, in the world.

SHIV'A

"Seven," referring to the seven days of mourning prescribed by Jewish law on the occasion of the death of a next-of-kin. Since the mourning ritual requires the mourners to be seated on low chairs, mourners are said "to *sit* Shiv'a."

SHMINI ATZERET

"The Eighth Day of Assembly," a Biblical festival following the Seven Days of Sukkot (see Glossary) and concluding it, but considered a festival in its own right.

SHOFAR

The Ram's Horn. The sounding of the Shofar is a principal ritual of Rosh Hashana, the New Year's Day.

SHUL, SHULE

Judeo-German for "Synagogue," literally meaning "school."

SIDDUR

The Prayerbook; literally, the "Arrangement."

SHULCHAN ARUCH

Literally, the "Set Table," a compendium of Jewish law by Rabbi Joseph Karo (1488 - 1575). It became the most authoritative code of Jewish law.

SUKKAH

"Tabernacle, Booth," the special structure to dwell in which is a mandatory observance of the Festival of Tabernacles, "Sukkot."

SUKKOT

The Biblical festival of "Tabernacles," observed in the fall as a thanksgiving festival and as a caution against complacency based on material security.

TAGORE, RABINDRANATH

Indian poet and philosopher (1869-1941).

TALLIT

A garment with four corners to which "Tzitzit" - "fringes to look at" - have been attached in fulfilment of the Biblical commandment (Numbers 15:38, 39). The Tallit is worn during daily morning prayers. A smaller four-cornered garment with Tzitzit, called "Tallit Katan - Small Tallit," is worn as part of a male's apparel. The "Tzitzit" is to serve as a reminder to fulfil God's commandments.

TALMUD

"The Learning" - the major work of Rabbinic law and lore, which received its final redaction in 500 C.E., and remains the basis of traditional Judaism. It is divided into tractates which are referenced in quotations.

TALMUD TORAH
An elementary Religious and Hebrew school for children.

TEFILLIN
"Phylacteries," leather boxes, containing four selections from the Torah attached with leather straps to the arm and the forehead in fulfilment of a Biblical commandment (Deuteronomy 6 and 11). Tefillin symbolize dedication to God's will in thought and action. The etymology of the word relates to "prayer."

TESHUVA
1. "Answer": a formal response to a question of Jewish law, "Responsum." 2. "Return," the process of Repentance, a basic concept in Jewish theology and ethics.

TISH'A B'AV
The "Ninth of Av," anniversary of the destruction of Jerusalem by the Romans in the year 70 C.E. and an annual day of mourning. "Av" is a month in the Jewish calendar occurring in the summer.

TORAH
"The Teaching." In its narrow sense, Torah refers to the Five Books of Moses, the Pentateuch. In its wider sense, it denotes the totality of Jewish religious literature authenticated by its ultimate derivation from Scripture. It also describes the content and spirit of Divine revelation.

TORAH PORTION
A section of the Torah assigned in the annual cycle of reading to a specific Shabbat, or to a Festival. The Hebrew word is "Sedra - Order," or "Perasha - Portion." In the Jewish calendar, a Shabbat is referred to by its "Perasha," thus "Shabbat Parshat Shemot" is the Shabbat on which the portion "Shmot" – the first portion of the Book of Exodus is read.

TREFA - see Kosher

TZADDIK
A righteous person; a traditional designation of an outstanding pious individual.

TZEDAKA
Literally "Righteousness," the word refers to acts of social righteousness usually described by the English word "charity," yet stressing the obligatory, rather than the voluntary nature of deeds of love, compassion and solidarity.

UJA
> United Jewish Appeal

YAD VASHEM
> Borrowed from Isaiah (55:5), the phrase which means "a hold and a name" is the name of the World Holocaust Memorial Museum and Research Center in Jerusalem.

YECKE
> Colloquial word of unknown origin for a German Jew.

YESHIVA
> A seminary of higher Jewish learning. The traditional curriculum of the Yeshiva concentrates on Talmud and Jewish law. At the completion of an appropriate period of study, a student may be ordained as Rabbi.

YIZKOR
> Popular name for the Memorial Service which is part of the liturgy of the Festivals. Worshippers recite prayers remembering deceased parents and other relatives.

YOM HA'ATZMA'UT
> Independence Day

YOM HASHO'A
> Holocaust Remembrance Day

YOM KIPPUR
> The "Day of Atonement" is the annual climax of the liturgical calendar and culminates a ten-day period of religious and moral regeneration beginning with Rosh Hashana, the New Year. Yom Kippur is marked by fasting, repentance and round-the-clock worship.

YORTZEIT
> From the German "Jahrzeit," the anniversary of a person's death observed by next-of-kin.

ZAIDA
> Yiddish for "grandfather."

The INDEX